PRAISE FOR WORSHIP JESUS: THE TABERNACLE

Worship of the Triune God is a serious and non-negotiable practice for all those who claim the name of Christ. In this timely and well-written book, Tracy Meola lays out a paradigm for worship that is drawn from the Old Testament yet points directly to the Savior. Solidly biblical, theologically astute and yet manifestly practical, *Worship Jesus: The Tabernacle* adds a whole new layer to prior discussions of what worship is and how it might look in our day and time. While some readers might disagree with parts of its argument, all will be instructed in this oh-so important aspect of our individual and corporate discipleship. Ms. Meola is to be commended for providing a fresh perspective on how we might worship the majestic and sovereign God Who has graciously called us to be His people.

— *Scott Wenig, PhD.*
Professor of Applied Theology;
Haddon Robinson Chair of Biblical Preaching
Denver Seminary

Jesus declares that the Father is seeking worshippers who will worship Him "in spirit and truth". Is there a blueprint for sinful people to come before a holy God? Tracy Meola offers God's instruction for tabernacle worship as a model for God's people today. In her careful and creative study she reminds us of foundational elements for the worship of God's people. She provides a valuable resource for personal, small group and community worship. Whether you are a full-time worship leader or not, you will find her questions and examples thought provoking.

— Randy MacFarland, DMin
Senior Professor of Pastoral Care and Leadership
Denver Seminary

In a time when everyone seems to have their own unique thought on worship, this fascinating book by Tracy Meola brings a fresh, and *new* old perspective to the worship of God by God's people. Her beautiful and thoughtful way of taking us through the foundations of worship as expressed by God's people in the Old Testament truly serves to call us to revive our contemporary thought and deed in worship with the most ancient; calling us to dig deeper through the elements of worship, and respond personally and corporately. I encourage you to both read this book, and use this book. Your eyes will be opened to God's *new* old blueprint for worship.

— Steven T. Taylor
Dean, School of Music
Colorado Christian University

Placing value on the biblical, historical, and theological foundations of worship, Tracy has given us a meaningful journey into Tabernacle worship that can inform our contemporary worship practices. That each chapter ends with the opportunity to "dig deeper," respond creatively, and voice a prayer makes the book extremely practical and allows this to truly become an experiential blueprint for worship.

— Nancy Nethercott, D. W.S.
Chaplain, The Robert E. Webber Institute for Worship Studies
Co-Director, IWS GROW Center

Worship Jesus: The Tabernacle by Tracy Meola is a highly introspective and remarkable read for any Christian who is serious about focusing on the foundational elements of worship. As the author emphasizes, these foundational elements "were designed to help us become a holy people who are set apart for God." Meola reveals how God's divine plan for worship was first shown in the Old Testament when God's people worshipped Him at the tabernacle in the wilderness. By gaining an in-depth understanding of the tabernacle, she believes we will readily see Jesus in every aspect of it, deepen our walk with Him and significantly enhance our worship experience. Certainly, something all believers should desire!

— Dick Bruso
Founder of Heard Above the Noise®
Professional Speaker and Author

Tracy personalizes the Tabernacle of Moses and its furnishings in a way that can bring spiritual significance to our lives in Christ Jesus. She reaches back into the instruction given to Moses for true worship and brings it forward into the New Testament. More importantly, she demonstrates how true worship is to be expressed today within the Body of Christ. In doing this, she lays out a progression in worship that results in an understanding of how it is that God desires to tabernacle with His people in this present day. She also offers some very practical application on how we are to exercise our priesthood by drawing from the words of the apostle Peter and the author of the book of Hebrews, (1 Peter 2:4-10; Hebrews 10).

— James Morel
Pastor and author of Destiny Seekers and
Two Sides of the Mountain

Tracy Meola has done her research! Worshipers, as well as those who lead them, will benefit from this insightful and detailed account of the Old Testament tabernacle and the ancient tools we have inherited from it that can help us worship.

— Danny Byram
Author,
Wallpaper Worship

WORSHIP
JESUS

THE TABERNACLE

WORSHIP
JESUS

THE TABERNACLE

TRACY MEOLA

ILLUMIFY
MEDIA.COM

WORSHIP JESUS:
THE TABERNACLE

Published by
Illumify Media Global
www.IllumifyMedia.com
"Let's Bring Your Book to Life!"

Library of Congress Control Number: 2019916638

Paperback ISBN: 978-1-964251-27-1
eBook ISBN: 978-1-964251-28-8

Typeset by Art Innovations (http://artinnovations.in/)
Cover design by Debbie Lewis
Illustrations by Courtney Mitchell

Printed in the United States of America

Contents

Foreword

*I*n the experience of any teacher or professor, there comes along an exceptional student. A student who listens with her eyes, questions with courage, speaks with conviction and learns beyond the requirements of the syllabus. For me, Tracy Meola was such a student.

Among evangelical churches there seems to be a genuine desire to improve the quality of corporate worship. Unfortunately, there is a growing number of believers who have grown up knowing little about biblical teaching on worship. Even fewer have studied what the Old Testament has to say regarding worship. I know of no book which offers a more concise and insightful investigation of worship as illustrated by the tabernacle than *Worship Jesus: The Tabernacle.*

Tradition holds that after a heartbreaking loss to end the season, coach Vince Lombardi held up a football before players who had lost their perspective of the core fundamentals of the game and said, "Gentlemen, *this* is a football!" What *is* worship? In the sea of books that seek to answer that question, what the church needs is a refreshing return to Scripture itself for a recovery of the biblical concepts of authentic worship. *Worship Jesus: The Tabernacle* offers that return. It's like Tracy Meola holds up the Bible and says,

"Church, *this* is worship!" The attentive reader will be immediately struck by the fact that *Worship Jesus: The Tabernacle* is permeated with Scripture, not merely through occasional quotations but with sustained exposition.

One of my favorite shows on television is *How It's Made*. In just a few fascinating minutes, this show explains how they get the cream in the middle of a Twinkie and why chocolate tastes so delicious and how mirrors do what they do. Maybe as a young child you too tore things apart to see how they worked. My life has been filled with disassembled (and only occasionally successfully reassembled) alarm clocks, cassette players (for those who remember), hair driers, and a transmission (that was truly a mistake). All of those adventures were driven by my curiosity to know how they worked and why. I had many aha moments as I discovered the hidden secrets below the surface. *Worship Jesus: The Tabernacle* is filled with aha moments. There will be moments when you will find yourself mumbling, *so that's what that means!*

One of those moments for me as I read her book was when Tracy wrote about the significance of the bronze altar in her section titled "Christ and the Altar." Tears filled my eyes as I read about the noisy little lamb that was led to the tabernacle on a rope. After placing a hand on the head of that bleating lamb, it was killed by the worshipper who brought it to pay for sin—the foolish things done. I was stunned by how cavalier I had become about the meaning of sacrifice and the gravity of my sin. I believe revival is born from a renewed awareness of the gravity of our sin.

Following a persuasive argument for why we should even bother studying Old Testament worship, Tracy Meola exegetes an often-overlooked parable in Hebrews 9 to show that the tabernacle provides the *blueprint* for worship. The book then offers a wonderful exegesis of how Christ is seen in the architecture, design, and furnishings of the tabernacle. The bronze altar, the bronze laver, the tabernacle tent, and the holy place furnishings all provide rich insight to a deeper understanding of worship.

Of particular significance is the emphasis of *nonverbal* elements of worship. Much of Protestant worship focuses on words. We act as if significance and importance are reserved for the spoken and written word. However, in worship we are by definition in the presence of mystery. Worship is multisensory and cannot be fully expressed exclusively to logical sentences. Worship is indeed about words, but it is also about movement, sounds, smells, music, symbols, and space.

Worship Jesus: The Tabernacle is not simply an academic exercise. At the close of each chapter there are discussion questions provided as well as practical application suggestions. As suggested by the author, *Worship Jesus: The Tabernacle* would be a wonderful study for any worship team. There is also an appendix that offers a sample tabernacle service.

The term *paradigmatic shift* has been often misunderstood. Deciding to eat somewhere different for lunch is not a shift in paradigms. The decision to remove the concept of lunch from our collective experience would qualify. After reading *Worship Jesus: The Tabernacle,* I believe that if evangelical worship would embrace what you are about to read, our churches would experience a true *paradigmatic shift* and God-sent revival! But enough of the overture! On to the main event.

— *Larry Lindquist, EdD*
Senior Professor of Leadership
Denver Seminary

Introduction

On Christmas Eve one year, my husband and I visited a church we had never before attended. As I sat there in the crowded room with hundreds of other people, I anxiously awaited to see how this church would bring us the message of the first coming of our Savior. In all fairness, what I most wanted was to enjoy a final "Silent Night" sung by candlelight as we all quietly contemplated the special night when Jesus, the Light of the World, was born. There is just something sweet about seeing the flame pass from candle to candle until the room glows—by far my favorite tradition during that time of year.

My experience was not the experience I had hoped for. During the course of the evening, one of the pastors admitted he wanted to take pictures of us, because he wanted to prove to his church consultant he could indeed fill this large room with people. He did just that, snapping pictures and selfies of and with us as he walked across the stage. I thought to myself, "Okay, this service can still be redeemed. He is simply one bad apple in the bunch."

However, another pastor got up and decided to share with us how he wanted us to partake in something which had always been on his bucket list—doing the wave in church. You know, when the crowd at a baseball or football game takes turns standing up and sitting down so it appears as a wave of motion moving around the stadium. Yes, we were asked to do the wave. In church. On Christmas Eve.

I understand some may read the above and think this might be a fun church to attend; however, my heart sunk. This had nothing to do with the message of Christmas, and it seemed those in charge simply wanted to pump up their own egos when they realized how many people were in their building that night. "Surely, *this* can't be what God desires from His church?" I thought.

At that point in my life I had been in church leadership long enough to know first impressions matter. I thought perhaps the church leadership were just not aware of how a new person might feel in their service. I sent an e-mail to the leaders of the church after the holiday season was over to share how I had felt as a newcomer in their church—as simply a number to fill in a seat and not a person. The response I received was that I just didn't understand what they were trying to do. I agree.

So what are we really trying to do in church? Many churches will cater their services toward a certain demographic or a particular culture. There are all types of gimmicks to draw in various people groups. To the leaders in the church, I have to ask what does *God* call us to do? Does He actually have a plan for our corporate worship times or are we free to do our own thing each time we gather for church? How are we to lead the people to Him in our services? What does He require of us? We often spend so much time trying to plan our services for those who aren't yet attending, that we do a disservice to those who are.

As a young worship leader, I looked to the New Testament to find instructions on how to order our worship because I figured it was the account of when the church was birthed. Surely it would be the best place to find how best to worship. I found all kinds of passages relating to worship, but I couldn't understand why God didn't have someone record an early church service in writing to give us some guidelines. Yes, we are to worship in spirit and in truth (John 4:23). Yes, we are to be extravagant in our worship (Luke 7:37-38). Jesus even sang a hymn (Matt. 26:30; Mark 14:26) after he instituted Communion. He also told us we are to love the Lord our God with all our heart, soul, mind, and strength—an act of worship (Mark 12:33). Aha! He was quoting Deuteronomy 6:5. Perhaps there was more in the Old Testament about worship than I had ever thought to consider.

Over the years, I have come to understand that God does indeed have a lot to say about His desires for us in our worship services. In fact, He gave us a service blueprint to follow, but it wasn't with the early Christian church in the book of Acts. It was established and recorded in the book of Exodus when He saved His people from harsh slavery in Egypt and led them into the wilderness to worship Him. Where did they worship God? In the tabernacle— the dwelling place of God as He accompanied His people in the wilderness.

Interestingly, the tabernacle not only points toward Jesus and gives us insight into corporate worship, but it is also a pattern of what is already in heaven! Hebrews 8:5 tells us that it was incredibly important for Moses to follow the instructions given for the building of the tabernacle. Not only was it important because it was to be God's dwelling place on earth with His people but also because it represented something already in existence in heaven! One day, we will see this place, and we will worship there as well. This is a place I want to understand.

Therefore, this book will be based on a little known parable found in the book of Hebrews (Hebrews 9) which sets the Old Testament tabernacle alongside the life and ministry of Jesus Christ. The writer of Hebrews *wanted* us to look back to understand how each of the elements (such as the bronze altar, the bronze laver, and the table of showbread) portrayed some aspect of the life and ministry of Jesus Christ. As we come to understand each of these elements, a blueprint for worship will emerge—a pattern God designed!

As you might guess, this is not your typical book about Christian worship. There are already many books written to define what worship is or to study different aspects of the expressions of worship (singing, prayer, acts of service, prophetic word). This book does not focus on any of those. Instead, it focuses on the *foundational elements* of worship. These are the things God established for us to celebrate and remember. They are the things we experience in our relationship with Him which cause us to want to express worship to God, such as God's holiness, His forgiveness, and His sanctifying process. In other words, we have an encounter with some aspect of God and respond in worship. Our expression comes through things like music, prayer, and studying the Word of God.

In order to understand God's plan we must look at the kind of worship God asked for from His people in the Old Testament as they worshiped Him at the tabernacle in the wilderness. These foundational elements of worship were designed to help us become a holy people who are set apart for God. We are to be holy because our God desires that of us (Lev. 19:2; 1 Pet. 1:15-16). You might wonder how the tabernacle and Jesus are related. It's a good question to ask and this is where the journey starts and the connections between Old and New Testament worship begins.

My hope is there are some of you reading this book who have the incredible gift and blessing from God to be an influence in the corporate worship of your church. We need to come back to our roots and understand worship from God's point of view and not simply look for what is most relevant, what feels good, or what will draw in the biggest crowds. We need to create services and experiences for the church that draws them to Christ and not create little gimmicks we hope will simply make the church a fun and more engaging place to be. It is my desire that this book will help our church leaders and our churches better understand this ancient Jewish heritage we have with regard to worship and to create moments for their congregations which tap into a worship service God designed thousands of years ago. This book is, by no means, offered in a way to suggest that the church *must* worship this way. It is, by all means, intended to be offered as a suggestion that will most likely enlighten and bring a deeper connection to our roots of worship. I'm glad you've chosen to join me on this journey.

1

No One is Exempt!

_W_orship is like a multi-faceted gemstone. You can approach it from a personal level or a corporate level. It can be described from a day to day perspective, a yearly cycle or a lifelong journey. We can look at the contrast between earthly worship and heavenly worship. It can be thought of in terms of various expressions, such as music, art, poetry, drama, and dance.

Before we even start to look at how God views worship, pause and see if you can define what worship is. How would you define it in your own life? How would you define it in the context of your church? What does it mean to worship? How are you most comfortable expressing worship to God? What expressions of worship are more challenging to you that you admire in others?

When it comes down to it, defining worship is not necessarily an easy thing to do because there is no easy answer. There are actually many beautiful definitions of worship given by a vast number of pastors, worship leaders, and scholars, and I won't attempt to add my own definition. However, I want us to recognize a common thread which seems to be a part of almost every definition of worship. Worship includes God revealing something to us and us responding to God.

It may or may not surprise you to hear that no one is exempt from worshipping. This covers all people everywhere! There is not one person, past, present, or future who does not or has not worshiped something or someone. At some point everyone evaluates the world around them and chooses to worship someone or something. God created everyone with the need to worship. In fact, everyone on earth at this very moment is worshipping something they value. Everyone worships; no one is exempt!

It is natural to focus ourselves and our energy toward something or someone we highly value. God designed us this way with the hope we would choose Him. However, some people value (or worship) money, sex, fame, power, and even other people. There are those who spend a great amount of time pursuing money, fame, or power. And then there are those who keep track of all the latest happenings of the superstars in Hollywood or the politicians in government. Those who are Muslim have chosen to worship and follow the teachings of Muhammad. Those who are Buddhists have chosen to worship and follow the teachings of Buddha. Those who are Christians have chosen to worship and follow the teachings of Jesus Christ—to value Him above all else. It is this last category—evangelical Christian worship—which will be addressed in this book.

It is important to understand, God has not made Himself distant from mankind and thus made it difficult to choose to worship Him. In fact, He has revealed Himself and made it quite easy for all people to find and worship Him. The apostle Paul tells us that *"since the creation of the world God's invisible qualities—his eternal power and divine nature—have been clearly seen, being understood from what has been made, so that people are without excuse"* (Rom. 1:20). We can easily look around and see there is a Creator. It is not by random chance that nature and humanity exists as it does. Creation has a plan, a design—and a Designer.

The beauty of our relationship with God is that He always initiates first! He reveals Himself in nature and gives us all plenty of reasons to come to Him, but He allows the decision to be ours. He always has and always will initiate a relationship with His creation, and we have no excuse not to recognize Him because the evidence of His presence is hard to ignore. He loves us so much that He freely offers Himself to us first; whether or not we receive and respond (express our worship) to His offer is a separate issue.

Foundational Elements of Worship

Sometimes, worship often ends up feeling like something we attend on Sunday morning. Corporate worship is something we are commanded to do, however, worship is so much more than attending a service once a week. It is not just an event that happens when the body gathers together for corporate worship, nor is it defined by a music style or type of songs sung in a corporate setting. It is not just prayer, contemplation, nor living a life focused on Christ. I would argue these are all *expressions* of worship based on an acceptance or understanding of *foundational elements* such as grace, mercy, love, forgiveness, holiness, and intimacy which are a part of God's design for worship. These elements are things we experience which God has designed for us to experience as we live in relationship with Him. They are there for us as we experience God. They all come together in a plan He alone established. Without choosing and ordering these elements as He did, we would never be welcomed into the presence of the One and only holy Creator of the universe.

Consider the life of a new believer. Christian worship begins as the result of an encounter with God during which the individual recognizes their need to repent and accept God's gift of salvation. They become aware they have sinned and are in need of God. This act of taking their eyes off of "self" and understanding God in a new way is the beginning of expressing Christian worship. It is the acknowledgement that there is something greater than self which needs to be valued or worshiped.

Offering our lives in surrender to God's will is the first expression of Christian worship. The foundational elements of repentance, forgiveness, God's holiness, and love have been experienced in a personal encounter with God. These elements are experienced in an extra personal way and an expression of worship comes in response. As one continues to have more experiences with God, expressions of gratitude, reverence, thanksgiving, and awe, for example, occur more frequently. Our expression or language of personal worship beings to expand and grow through things like music, prayer, contemplation, or serving the poor and homeless in the name of Christ. As our worship expression grows and expands, our holiness (becoming more Christlike and less worldly) increases.

God established these foundational elements of worship so we might have a relationship with Him. He laid out everything in great detail and designed the blueprint for how we experience Him and how He desires to be worshiped. In fact, as we look at some of these elements which began in the Old Testament, it should become clear that when it comes to the foundation of worship, all of the church's many denominations may have much more in common than they realize. While our *expressions* of worship vary greatly (and tend to cause all kinds of problems and arguments among different denominations), the *foundational elements* do not change.

Too often, the Christian church will look only as far back as the book of Acts as its model for our modern-day church. However, we must remember early Christian worship was first practiced by Jewish believers. Their context for worship came from a Jewish faith, and their worship practices came from their understanding of the traditions and events which took place in the Jewish temple in Jerusalem as they worshipped a Jewish Messiah.

As New Testament believers in Christ, we need to delve further back than the book of Acts and the formation of the early Christian church to truly understand where our worship traditions come from. It was God who laid out exceptionally detailed plans for worship as He called on the Israelites to construct the Old Testament tabernacle. Since God's pattern is a shadow of what is already in heaven, we have the opportunity to understand God's blueprint for worship and experience it both corporately and personally as we look forward to heaven.

Jesus and the Parables

If you have been studying the Scriptures for any length of time, you have probably read many of the parables Jesus told His followers. We don't use the term *parable* in our contemporary language, but it might be helpful to think of parables simply as stories. They are stories or illustrations used to teach some element of God's truth, usually by comparing or contrasting two or more things. The parables Jesus told compared two or more things in order to display some element of biblical truth.

Jesus shared many truths and much wisdom with His followers over the course of His ministry through parables. We see His wisdom in the parable of the sower (Matt. 13:1-23), the parable of the mustard seed (Mark 4:30-34), the parable of the workers in the vineyard (Matt. 20:1-16), and the parable of the good Samaritan (Luke 10:25-36), for instance. In these illustrations, Jesus sought to engage the people to understand truth using stories they could relate to which were relevant for their time and place in history.

For example, in the parable of the sower found in Matthew 13:1-23, Jesus talks about the ways in which the Word of God is received or takes root in the hearts of mankind. As seed (the Word of God) is sown, it will be received in one of three manners:

1. The one who hears the Word of God but does not take it seriously is like seed sown on rocky ground. Just like that seed, the Word of God never really penetrates the heart of the man or woman, and it never truly takes root.

2. The one who hears the Word of God and allows it to enter into their heart but remains self-focused is like the seed that falls among the thorns. The seed may take root, but it will be very sickly and never bear fruit because of the weeds and thorns constantly threatening to choke the life out of it. The Word of God is partially understood and accepted but is never truly cultivated and never becomes mature and healthy.

3. The one who hears of the Word of God and allows it to change their life is like the seed which has fallen on good soil. It is easy for the seed to take root and become a healthy, fruit-bearing plant. The Word of God penetrates the heart, takes root, and a beautiful, healthy, fruit-bearing life is the result.

In the above example, Jesus took the idea of sowing seeds

because the people lived in an agrarian society and then compared this action to accepting the Word of God and living a life following God's Word. While we can appreciate the necessity of having well cultivated soil for good crops to grow, a farmer or gardener might understand this message in ways those of us who are not farmers or gardeners may miss. Perhaps this is why Jesus used a variety of parables. Each of these stories will speak differently to us in different ways.

Jesus and the Parable of Hebrews 9

As we turn to the focus of this study, we turn to a little known and often overlooked parable from the book of Hebrews. For those who only equate parables with Jesus' teaching, it may surprise you to know there are other parables in Scripture. Hebrews 9 is an example. It is not a parable Jesus spoke, but is instead a parable about Him.

In this passage, we see how the author of Hebrews chose to compare the life and ministry of Jesus Christ with something the Jews could relate to—the tabernacle. The tabernacle was the tent structure that accompanied the Israelites through the wilderness after the exile from Egypt. God came to dwell among His people in this tabernacle tent. It was their sanctuary and God's home in the desert of the Sinai.

Before we go further, let me clarify one thing. The tabernacle no longer existed in the time of Jesus because a temple had been built in Jerusalem to replace it hundreds of years before Jesus. King David actually set out to build the temple as a replacement for the tabernacle during his reign as king, but he was a warrior and a man of bloodshed so God told the king that his son Solomon would build a house for Him instead (1 Chron. 28:5-7). After Solomon's temple was destroyed during the Babylonian captivity, the temple was then rebuilt and expanded upon by Herod. It is this second temple which stood during the time of Christ.

Both the tabernacle and the temple served the same purpose so these terms can be used interchangeably when speaking of their ministry and purpose. They both served as the seat of daily life for God's people, although at different times in history. They were also both seen as the dwelling place of God among His people. The priests served God in the same manner in both the tabernacle and the temple. The tabernacle was simply the mobile tent while the temple was built in Jerusalem as a permanent structure. As one would expect, the fixed temple in Jerusalem was a much grander structure, which surely dazzled the senses of those who visited, although the tabernacle was filled with riches as well!

You might wonder why the author didn't simply compare Jesus to the temple in Jerusalem since that was what was in existence at the time of Christ. There are a number of theories as to why. The first is that by the time the book of Hebrews was written, Stephen had already been stoned for criticizing the temple. The author may have wanted to distance himself from stirring up trouble. Therefore, the tabernacle was used as the example instead. Since the primary function is much the same and the people would have understood what he meant, it might have given the author a comparison without immediately turning Jews away in anger.

Another theory has to do with the amount of detailed instruction given for the tabernacle in the Old Testament writings. All those details are incredibly important because God said the tabernacle was to be laid out following the heavenly pattern already in existence. There are some instructions regarding the temple, but by far, the instructions given for the tabernacle help us see a clearer picture of what was involved in the construction.

Regardless, Hebrews 9:1-4 sets the scene by giving a brief reminder of the layout of the tabernacle. It seems those to whom the author was writing would have understood this because in verse 5 he wrote, "But we cannot discuss these things in detail now" as if he's saying, "you already know these things; let us move on." This is perhaps one of the most frustrating verses in the Bible! Wouldn't we have *loved* to hear a New Testament writer explain the ark of the covenant and the glory of God from his point of view? Nevertheless, he quickly moves on, briefly mentioning the duties of the priests including the need for the high priest to enter into the Most Holy Place once a year to make a blood offering for all the sins the people had committed (Hebrews 9:6-8). Then we come to Hebrews 9:9: "*This is an illustration for the present time,* indicating that the gifts and sacrifices being offered were not able to clear the conscience of the worshiper."

If you look at Hebrews 9:9 carefully, you might notice the tabernacle is described as an *illustration.* Some translations use the word *symbol.* Either way, the original Greek word used here may look familiar in its English transliteration: *parabole.* It is where we get our English word *parable.* The passage immediately following this (Heb. 9:10-28) talks about the blood of Christ serving as the atonement sacrifice of the new covenant. In other words, Christ has been disclosed as the way into the Most Holy Place. It was the blood of Christ, and not the blood of animals, that went beyond the veil into the Most Holy Place as Christ was sacrificed as the atonement for the sins of all mankind.

The tabernacle, its purpose and the priest's duties there, can and should be viewed alongside the life of Jesus—our ultimate

High Priest. This parable allows us to see the tabernacle in great detail and connect it with who Jesus is and what He did for us. It is symbolic and shows us how we can receive forgiveness and have the privilege to *"approach the throne of grace with confidence, so that we may receive mercy and find grace to help us in our time of need"* (Heb. 4:16). While the first tabernacle was standing, all the rules, rituals, and regulations surrounding it were in effect, but with the coming of Christ, a new tabernacle was among us. "The Word became flesh and made his dwelling among us. We have seen his glory, the glory of the one and only Son, who came from the Father, full of grace and truth" (John 1:14).

The word *dwelling* in this verse is a Greek word which means "to pitch" or "live in a tent." Some translations actually translate this word as "tabernacle." In other words, the first tabernacle is no longer necessary because God Himself came in the flesh to live among mankind. The writer of Hebrews wanted to make this connection for the Jewish people—the incarnation of God was no longer in the temple. The tabernacle (and by extension the temple) were always meant to be clues pointing forward toward the coming Christ. Christ came to replace the tabernacle (and the temple by extension). God's manifest presence was no longer in the temple. He was found out in the streets of Jerusalem in the person of Jesus Christ.

This parable connects Jesus with Old Testament worship in significant ways. It is the bridge between understanding ancient Israel and their sacrificial system and Jesus and His fulfillment of the sacrificial system. New Testament worship is not about putting the perfect music set together to emphasize the pastor's sermon. It is not about creating a fun or appealing atmosphere. It is about creating a space where people can come to experience God through things like repentance, forgiveness, cleansing, communion, holiness, and intimacy—the foundational elements of worship.

The tabernacle is God's blueprint for worship. When we follow His pattern, He reveals what repentance and sanctification truly are. He reveals His grace, mercy, and offer of forgiveness. He reveals how we are to come as a holy people before Him. He reveals how we are to continue to live in right relationship with Him. He reveals Himself, and we respond with expressions of worship. This was all accomplished in the design of the tabernacle—a blueprint of the heavenly sanctuary.

Somehow along the way, the church has forgotten this extremely rich parable for understanding what God had in mind for our worship service all along. So often in our church services today, we welcome people in a manner similar to welcoming people into the outer courts of the temple. Unfortunately, we often try to dive quickly into the Holy of Holies, bypassing the richness of everything in between the outer court and the intimate Holy of Holies.

Let us pause and examine what we miss when we rush into God's presence. In the next chapter we will look at the importance of knowing the why behind our worship.

2

Why Study
Old Testament Worship?

Some people like to dismiss the Old Testament as a scary time when God smote people for seemly no reason at all. I understand their aversion to the ancient days and their desire to discard certain Old Testament worship practices altogether because they were exercised during a time when people were living under the law and not under grace. This is perhaps the number one reason most people reject Old Testament worship practices. It is unfortunate this happens, but it is understandable because there often seems to be a difficult gap to bridge between the Old and New Testament. It is important to address some of the arguments against and then for Old Testament worship practices before continuing forward in this study.

Arguments Against Old Testament Worship Practices

Old Testament worship can feel exceptionally awkward and confusing to a New Testament believer. The Old Testament was a time of animal sacrifice and rituals, and it can be hard to relate to something so foreign. We have a vastly different worship experience in our church today which seems far removed from the things we read in the Old Testament. Let us first look at some of these objections to Old Testament worship.

John 1 tells us the person of Jesus Christ became the dwelling place of God on earth. So if Jesus is the ultimate fulfillment, some may argue the sacrificial system used in the Old Testament ended with the coming of Christ, and there is no way the actual practices of animal sacrifice, burning incense and the many other rules, rituals, feasts and festivals the Jews were obligated to follow have any implication on today's contemporary worship. We are not required to bring animal sacrifices nor give any of the many required offerings the Jews had to give on a regular basis. The Old Testament is simply filled with old rules, traditions, and laws that do not apply to the New Testament church. In fact, the Old Testament could be viewed as simply one giant book of rules and regulations we are not required to follow since we live under the grace of the New Covenant and not the law of the Old Covenant. None of these things are relevant for today. We might ask is there really any reason to go back and do an in-depth study on the tabernacle? Why would we spend our time studying a worship style that is no longer necessary since Christ is the fulfillment? Wouldn't we be better off studying the life of Christ?

Still others may argue there is really no reason to study Old Testament worship because it is simply so old and irrelevant. There are many early instructions for worship found in the Torah (Genesis through Deuteronomy), but they were not only written to the Jews, these books are thought to have been written in part, if not in full, by Moses and he's a pretty old dude! In fact, all of the Old Testament books were written long before the time of Christ. The most recent Old Testament books were probably written in the early 400s BC—four hundred years before Christ even lived on this earth! The thought is that the Old Testament is fine for the Jews to study because it deals with the Jewish people, but we follow Christ, and since the Old Testament was written well before the beginning of the Christian church, we should really focus on the New Testament books and the birth of the Christian church.

Lastly, since the Christian church began after Christ was resurrected, His words and His life are where we should focus, some say. Why would we need to look at the Old Testament for clues to practicing Evangelical Christian worship today? The Old Testament deals with the Jews and their rules, not Christians. Jesus says He came to fulfill the law, so we need to simply look at Jesus and His teachings. The things most relevant to us as Christ followers, will be the teachings of Christ. As mentioned earlier, we live under grace and not under the law as the Old Testament people did.

While these arguments *against* studying Old Testament worship are all certainly understandable, there are also arguments *for* studying Old Testament worship that are equally valid and should be considered. Taking time to understand the Old Testament will only enrich our understanding of the New Testament.

Arguments for Old Testament Worship Practices

1. Jesus Says the Scriptures Are About Him

This first point should be prefaced with the following passage spoken by the apostle Paul as he instructed Timothy: "All Scripture is God-breathed and is useful for teaching, rebuking, correcting and training in righteousness, so that the servant of God may be thoroughly equipped for every good work" (2 Tim. 3:16-17). When Paul was speaking of "all Scripture," it is important to note the New Testament was still in its early stages and what we know as the term *Scripture* in the New Testament, was actually referring to the Old Testament writings.

The apostle Paul was an incredibly devout Jew (Acts 23:6), a Pharisee in particular. Pharisees were known to understand Scripture (Old Testament) inside and out and to be extraordinarily strict and legalistic in keeping all the laws, customs, and rituals prescribed in them. With this background *and* a saving knowledge in Christ, Paul still proclaimed *all* Scripture (Old and New Testament alike) is from God and useful for teaching, rebuking, correcting, and training. If we believe this passage of Paul's, we must recognize both the Old and New Testaments are valid for us to understand as a part of our faith and as an expression of worship.

Now it is clear that Jesus came to fulfill the law, but we have to remember what the full verse says: "Do not think that I have come to abolish the Law or the Prophets; I have not come to abolish them but to fulfill them" (Matt. 5:17). Jesus said He did not come to overthrow or destroy the Old Testament law but to completely fulfill the law. The Greek word for fulfill is pléroó (play-ro'-o), which means "to make full" or "to fill to capacity." There is no connotation of having been done away with. Instead Jesus seems to imply that when we look at the Old Testament alongside His life, we will understand to the fullest what the Old Testament is really saying. He does not desire we discard the Old Testament but that we would instead understand it to its fullest. There is a tremendous richness to studying the Old Testament and when we view the Old Testament through the life of Christ, we can more fully understand the Old Testament laws, rituals, and festivals found there.

Consider also, the words Jesus spoke of Himself to the Jewish leaders: "You study the Scriptures diligently because you think that in them you have eternal life. These are the very Scriptures that testify about me, yet you refuse to come to me to have life" (John 5:39-40). We might actually completely agree with this verse without really thinking it through. We can look in our Bible and find all kinds of Scriptures about Christ. The entire New Testament is filled with His teachings and His words. Just as I mentioned with Paul above, we must remember Jesus was a Jew and the Scriptures Jesus speaks of are the Old Testament Scriptures. These are the Scriptures the Jewish leaders studied. Upon examination we see much of the Old Testament is filled with stories that foreshadow or point the reader to the person of Jesus Christ. Those Jewish leaders just couldn't see it. If we read our Old Testament with this in mind, surely we will find things in the Old Testament to enlighten our understanding and enrich our worship of Him.

2. Jesus is Foreshadowed in the Old Testament

There are two terms that are good to be familiar with: type and shadow (or foreshadow). To foreshadow something is to use an object, a story, or an idea as a representation of something yet to come. To foreshadow is to give an indication or hint that there is something else coming. Much of the Old Testament was written to foreshadow Jesus Christ. It was written before the time of Christ but is meant to be an indication and representation of the life of Jesus Christ, although He came much later in history.

Think about what a shadow is for a moment. A shadow is formed when an object blocks the portion of light shining on the object. A shadow looks like the object, but it isn't the object. The object is real; the shadow is a representation. When God gives us a shadow of something, it is meant to point us forward to something real and yet to be fulfilled. We might see the shape of the object, but do not see it in full. The shadow is never the ultimate fulfillment but is simply an indication there is a real object present.

The term type is also good to understand in its Old Testament context. When we say something is a type in the Old Testament, we are saying it refers to an event, a person, or a story which actually happened and is fulfilled in the New Testament. A type often foreshadowed or pointed toward some aspect of God's truth as we read about it in the New Testament. Let us consider a few examples for a moment.

Romans 5:14 tells us Adam served as a type of Christ. Adam had a place in history and yet foreshadowed the redemption Christ brought. Through Adam's one act of disobedience, sin entered the world. Likewise, through one act of obedience to the Father, Christ redeemed mankind. Adam is a type of Christ and foreshadowed or pointed us toward Christ. Adam was not Christ but was a shadow of what was going to take place through Christ.

The story of Abraham and the sacrifice of Isaac is another example of a type and foreshadow of Christ. Like Christ, Isaac was to be an innocent sacrifice at the hands of his father. Abraham even placed the wood upon Isaac to carry up to the place of the sacrifice (Gen. 22:6) just as the cross was placed upon and carried by Christ to the place of His sacrifice (John 19:17). We can see parallels between Abraham and God the Father giving up His Son, Jesus Christ, as a sacrifice. We can see parallels between Isaac and Christ as the innocent sufferers. The ultimate fulfillment in the story is found in Jesus much later in history.

Interestingly, the commandments given on the mountain to Moses along with the commands regarding the building of the tabernacle, were given to point the people toward something yet to take place. Following the law and all the rules of the Old Testament were never meant to be their "salvation." The law was given to guide Israel on how to live as God's holy people set apart from the nations. The law was also given to point them to something greater yet to come. The writer of Hebrews gives us this insight: "The law is only a shadow of the good things that are coming—not the realities themselves. For this reason it can never, by the same sacrifices repeated endlessly year after year, make perfect those who draw near to worship" (Heb. 10:1). As New Testament believers, we have the privilege of seeing the fulfillment of the law in Christ!

We will see the tabernacle did exactly this same thing. It served as a type and foreshadow of Christ. The tabernacle was a real object in the Old Testament. Its purpose at the time it was erected among the people of Israel was to serve as God's dwelling place. At the same time, it actually serves as a visual representation of the life and ministry of Christ. It was originally built to help God's people understand how they were to engage with God. Primarily for the Jews of the Old Testament, the spiritual implications of the tabernacle is for both Jew and Gentile believers today as well.

3. We Are Grafted In

Before the Reformation and before the many different denominations, the church has been divided. It has been divided since the beginning, about two thousand years ago. The division back then was between Gentile believers and Jewish believers. One need only to look back at the events of the Jerusalem Council (Acts 15) to see there were serious disagreements about the process the Gentile Christians had to undergo to become a part of God's people. That divide still exists today.

Before moving into this point, I need to clarify some definitions because the distinctions between them are very important. Gentile Christians (Gentile Christ followers, Christians, believers) are those who do not have any natural Jewish heritage or DNA but who have come to faith in Christ and are now a part of God's people because of Christ. Jewish believers are called Messianic Jews. They are those who are part of a remnant chosen by God who have both a Jewish heritage and also believe in Christ as their Messiah and Savior. Sometimes the terminology used to describe them today is completed Jew because they were born Jewish but at some point in their lives they have also come to faith in the Messiah: Jesus Christ. There is also a subgroup here that you can call the Messianic Gentiles. This describes those who have no Jewish heritage but who acknowledge Christ *and* follow God's feasts and festivals alongside the Messianic Jews.

One of the primary differences between Messianic Jews and Gentile Christians revolves around their worship practices. Messianic Jews choose to follow many of the Jewish traditions which have been a part of their Jewish heritage since the book of Genesis. They are Christian in the sense that they believe Jesus is the Messiah (although they prefer to speak His name as Mary might have, calling Him Yeshua), but they understand the foreshadowing of Christ in the feasts and festivals commanded by God in Leviticus 23. They chose to follow these traditions rather than the church holidays (namely Christmas and Easter), which were fully developed a few hundred years after Christ.

However, as Christ followers we are all (Messianic Jew and Gentile Christian) God's chosen people, and yet we don't tend to acknowledge one another. There are some in the church who arrogantly think only Gentile believers are the bride of Christ. In the same manner, some Messianic Jews are not immune from arrogance as they claim their Jewish birthright gives them greater privilege over Gentile believers, Messianic or not. The apostle Paul (a Jew turned Messianic Jew) breaks down all the divisions:

> So in Christ Jesus you are all children of God through faith, for all of you who were baptized into Christ have clothed yourselves with Christ. There is neither Jew nor Gentile, neither slave nor free, nor is there male and female, for you are all one in Christ Jesus. If you belong to Christ, then you are Abraham's seed, and heirs according to the promise. (Galatians 3:26-29)

Another passage to help understand how we have all become one body and can call ourselves heirs of Abraham is found in Romans. It is an especially valuable study for all those who come to a saving knowledge in Christ whether Jew or Gentile. In this passage, Paul wrote to Gentiles and taught them to understand how God's chosen people were no longer just Jews but now included them as well because of Christ's work on the cross.

As a Jew, Paul knew exactly what it meant to be part of God's chosen people because he was born a Jew. After an incredible encounter with God, however, Paul was instructed to go to the Gentiles and teach them that they are also be a part of God's people. To explain this to the Gentiles, he uses the imagery of two different olive trees. A pruned and well-cared-for tree represents the Jews and a wild olive tree represents the Gentiles. In his analogy some of the branches from the well-cared-for tree were broken off and some from the wild olive tree were broken off of their tree and grafted into the well-cared-for tree:

> If some of the branches have been broken off, and you, though a wild olive shoot, have been grafted in among the others and now share in the nourishing sap from the olive root, do not boast over those branches. If you do, consider this: You do not support the root, but the root supports you. You will say then, "Branches were broken off so that I could be grafted in." Granted. But they were broken off because of unbelief, and you stand by faith. Do not be arrogant, but be afraid. For if God did not spare the natural branches, He will not spare you either. (Romans 11:17-21)

In other words, what Paul was saying was there is a well-cared for olive tree (Jewish in nature) and the root of this tree is Jesus Christ—a Jew. Along with this root come all the traditions, festivals, feasts, and customs uniquely Jewish in practice. At the time of Christ's crucifixion, there were some Jews who were cut off of this olive tree because of their unwillingness to see Jesus Christ as the true Messiah. Within a short amount of time, God began to graft in new branches: Gentiles who put their trust in Jesus Christ as the resurrected Messiah.

It is so important to understand the Christian church was not a newly planted tree that grew from the root of a resurrected Messiah but was instead grafted into a tree already in existence! The birth of the Christian church was not in the book of Acts; it simply became grafted into something already alive and well—the well-cultivated olive tree of God's original chosen people of Israel!

There are not two separate trees. There is only one tree—one body of believers—and the root of that tree is a Jewish Messiah.

The point of all of this is that as Gentile Christians, we should understand our heritage is found in a Jewish root. We are grafted into the Jewish olive tree of God's chosen people. This olive tree consists of Jews who have accepted Jesus as their Messiah and Gentiles who have done the same. To understand more about the nature of this pruned olive tree, we must look into the Old Testament to appreciate the Jewish root that we are connected to. As we dig deeper, we will see the commonality between Old Testament and New Testament worship, and it will bring Jewish and Gentile worship onto the same playing field in order to show how very much we actually have in common.

4. We Are Part of God's Royal Priesthood

It's not necessarily natural to think of ourselves as holy, royal priests, but when we come to Christ, that is exactly what we are! Consider this passage in Peter's letter to the believers:

> As you come to him, the living Stone—rejected by humans but chosen by God and precious to him—you also, like living stones, are being built into a spiritual house to be a holy priesthood, offering spiritual sacrifices acceptable to God through Jesus Christ. . . . But you are a chosen people, a royal priesthood, a holy nation, God's special possession, that you may declare the praises of him who called you out of darkness into his wonderful light. (1 Peter 2:4-5, 9)

You may have read or heard this passage many times, but have you ever really stopped to think about what it means? The term "royal" might bring to mind images of England's royal family: Queen Elizabeth, Prince Harry, or Prince William. But what about the term "priesthood"? For those who have not spent much time in a liturgical church, the term *priest* might be a little uncomfortable, and so we may have chosen to automatically translate this word into "pastor" instead.

It is important not to try to translate this passage into something comfortably contemporary or relevant to our understanding of a royal priest, but instead we should look at this verse in the context it was written. With this in mind, did you catch what was really being said in the last verse? In verse 9, Peter says we are *already* a royal priesthood!

To put this in context, it is important to note this passage was most likely written in the early AD 60s. The temple in Jerusalem was still standing and the priesthood was still not only in effect, but the priests were still serving in the temple. The people who received this letter from Peter had an understanding of what being a priest in the temple was all about.

So what does this term "royal priesthood" mean and what did the priests actually do in the Jerusalem temple? If we are already part of God's royal priesthood, what does this mean for us today? I propose we must go to the Old Testament and study the early priesthood appointments made by God for the answer and these are found in the context of the tabernacle.

5. We Are God's Temple

Paul lays it out clearly in his letter to the Corinthians: "Don't you know that you yourselves are God's temple and that God's

Spirit dwells in your midst?" (1 Cor. 3:16). As with the previous point, you may have heard this verse many times, but what does it really mean? Most of us don't attend a temple service, so we might also automatically translate this as being God's "church" without giving it much thought. It's easy to jump to the end of the verse and recognize God lives within us. That may feel comfortable and is not too difficult for most of us to grasp, but are we simply a structure (like the temple) where God lives? Why are we called God's temple? What happened at the temple in Jerusalem that would give Paul reason to compare us to a temple?

Again, I think it is important not to try to translate this verse into something contemporary or relevant for our time, but to look at it in the context in which it was written. There were a variety of things that happened in the temple during Paul's time. Some of the rituals at first glance may feel odd and irrelevant, such as the sacrifice of animals, but as with many things in the Old Testament, they are meant to serve as types or foreshadows and point us toward something else.

We are now God's living temple. He is no longer in a structure built by man. *We* are the structure—the place where God now dwells. As His living temples, we ought to know who we truly are. There are many instructions regarding the purpose of the tabernacle and temple in the Bible and the ministry that happened in them. In fact, there are references to the tabernacle or temple in more than fifty chapters of the Bible. God has given us much guidance to understand our purpose as His living temple. We just need to search it out—beginning with the tabernacle.

3

Laying the Foundation

efore diving into understanding the tabernacle itself, we need to look at the context and lay a foundation for understanding the bigger picture. In the early part of the book of Exodus, we see God chose Moses as the man He would work through to bring salvation to His people. Time and time again, Moses delivered the Word of God to Pharaoh and asked him to release the Hebrew slaves, so they might worship God in the wilderness. After Pharaoh and the Egyptians had dealt with plague upon plague, he finally gave in and released God's people (Ex. 12:31-33).

Think about this scene from the point of the average Egyptian. As an Egyptian, you would have been on the receiving end of all of the plagues that had struck your land, your animals, and your family. The infestation of pests, an abundance of frogs that got in everything, hail that killed all the crops, and painful boils and blisters that caused agony—all because your Pharaoh would not release the slaves to go worship their God. It's not too hard to imagine you would most likely have known the God of the Israelite slaves had been testing Pharaoh over and over again. If you were an Egyptian owner of slaves, you probably weren't too thrilled with your slaves either! Their powerful God was the instigator of all the havoc in your life. You would probably be quite happy when you heard that Pharaoh finally told those foreign slaves to leave.

Scripture tells us when Pharaoh gave the word to leave, the Egyptians *urged* the Hebrews to leave quickly. They were fed up and feared the Hebrew God would strike them all dead if they did not leave (Ex. 12:33). The people of God left Egypt in such a hurry they had no time to even prepare a meal to take with them. They were simply to gather their families, their children, their flocks and herds, and probably their most treasured possessions and leave. I can relate to a little of what they must have felt like.

My husband and I lived in the mountains of Colorado for many years, and a number of years ago we had many forest fires during the spring and early summer. Our home was threatened on more than one occasions by these fires. One time the fire department came around and evacuated everyone in our neighborhood. We had only two hours to pack up and leave. For some, two hours was actually a luxury! When you are faced with the possibility of losing your home and only have two hours, what do you take? We had no children other than our furry feline companions, which we put into the car along with our clothing, some toiletries, important documents, and some things that held sentimental value. There was no guarantee we were going to have a home to come back to and feared most of our possessions would burn.

I image this is somewhat like what God's people experienced except they *knew* they would not be returning. This was it. They were leaving with whatever they could carry with them. Fortunately for my husband and me, we were able to return home.

The people were finally free to worship God. Shortly after this departure from Egypt, God gave Moses instructions on how to build a tabernacle, so He would have a place to dwell in the midst of His people as they worshiped Him. Interestingly, in the giving of these instructions, God was also giving Moses a glimpse of the blueprint of His dwelling place which already existed in heaven: "They serve at a sanctuary that is a copy and shadow of what is in heaven. This is why Moses was warned when he was about to build the tabernacle: 'See to it that you make everything according to the pattern shown you on the mountain' " (Heb. 8:5).

When it came time to gather the items necessary to create this dwelling place, God also instructed Moses to have the people bring forward some very specific offerings:

> The LORD said to Moses, "Tell the Israelites to bring me an offering. You are to receive the offering for me from everyone whose heart prompts them to give. These are the offerings you are to receive from them: gold, silver and bronze; blue, purple and scarlet yarn and fine linen; goat hair; ram skins dyed red and another type of durable leather; acacia wood; olive oil for the light; spices for the anointing oil and for the fragrant incense; and onyx stones and other gems to be mounted on the ephod and breast piece. Then have them make a sanctuary for me, and I will dwell among them. Make this tabernacle and all its furnishings exactly like the pattern I will show you." (Exodus 25:1-9)

Since it is clear the departure out of Egypt was quick, this might lead many to wonder why the Hebrew slaves had gold, silver, and fine linen or how they came to acquire these things. What's interesting about this story is God made sure they actually carried everything for the tabernacle into the wilderness with them as they left Egypt.

God made the Egyptians "favorably disposed" toward the Israelites. They simply had to ask the Egyptians for these precious items and the Egyptians willingly gave them what they asked for (Ex. 12:31-36). Fascinating! We see a people who were bitterly enslaved now being given precious gifts by the same people who had enslaved them as they were departing their land! The Egyptian people feared the God of Israel and wanted to be done with Him. As a result, well over one ton of gold was collected as well as nearly four tons of silver and about three tons of bronze in addition to the necessary animal skins, precious gemstones, and fine linens.

While Moses was on the mountain of God receiving the instructions for the tabernacle and for living as God's holy people, the people grew impatient for his return. Moses took longer than they expected. They feared something happened to Moses and decided to take matters into their own hands. At this point, you may be familiar with the story of the golden calf.

The surrounding pagan nations would often create idols within which they would invite their gods to inhabit and it is likely that was what the Israelites had in mind when they decided to fashion a statue (a golden calf) for their God who had just delivered them from Egypt. God had already made it clear He intended to personally dwell among the people and not in something crafted by their hands. This was certainly an incredible abomination to the Lord. He had just provided abundantly for His people as He saved them out of Egypt, and then they resorted to trying to worship the way the pagan nations did. God became angry, Moses interceded, and destroyed the statue. He ground the gold into powder, sprinkled it on water, and made the Israelites consume it (Ex. 32:19-20).

What is the significance of this in relation to the tabernacle? Even in God's anger, we see incredible mercy and provision. He foreknew this would happen, and yet He allowed the people not only to collect the full ton of gold needed for the tabernacle but enough to create the golden calf as well. God didn't just provide exactly what was needed to create His dwelling place. He provided in great abundance. Even after their failure, they still had plenty to do as God commanded. God provided in spite of their failures.

The Israelite Camp

Consider all the stories you have ever learned about the Israelites wandering in the desert for forty years. What do you think of when you picture them in the wilderness? What did the wilderness look like? How do you picture God in their midst? What do the priests do there? Stop reading for a moment and take time to really visualize what the Israelite camp might look like to you.

Maybe you have a picture in mind. Maybe you have no idea what I'm talking about. Personally, I used to picture an incredibly barren desert with a fence of some sort surrounding sacred objects with millions of people camping in tents nearby. I imagined the priests offering sacrifices and whatever else priests did—something to do with bread, lighting candles, perhaps some singing, playing musical instruments, and I'm not sure what else. The ark of the covenant was there in a place called the Holy of Holies, and there was an altar for burnt offerings somewhere in the midst of all of this. I could recall something about a menorah, a table with bread on it, and an altar for incense, but I didn't know much more beyond

that. I didn't know where any of these objects were located or even
what the tabernacle was exactly.

As far as size goes, I always guessed since there were possibly
millions of people wandering the desert, the tabernacle had to be
at least the size of a large shopping mall, perhaps even the size of a
stadium. I was not sure how everything fit together, but I figured
it must have been huge! I was so wrong. Did you do better than I
did? As we continue the journey, your picture will become clearer.

The wilderness of the Sinai Peninsula is incredibly barren.
If you travel over there today, you will see there is literally no
vegetation. None at all. There are times you may even feel like you
are on the moon. It is that barren! I grew up in the southwest, the
desert region of the United States, and it is filled with an abundance
of vegetation compared with the deserts of the Middle East.

As for the number of people in the wilderness? There is great
debate over the actual number. We won't go into great detail here,
but I will introduce you to the issue a bit. If we take the literal
number of all the Israelites able to serve in Israel's army, we find
there were 603,550 men according to the census taken in Numbers
1:46. There are some scholars who take this literally, and if you
add children, spouses, parents, and grandparents into the mix,
there may have been approximately three million people in the
desert; that's a fairly good-sized, modern-day city. In contrast to
this number and at the writing of this text, Jerusalem's metro area
currently has a population of slightly below 1.3 million people (of
all nationalities).

Other scholars disagree with this number because
Deuteronomy 7:1 says when the Israelites enter the land they are to
possess, they will drive out seven nations larger and stronger than
them. Archeologically, it does not appear there were that many

nations with more than two to three million people. These scholars would argue that the translation of many of the census numbers in the book of Numbers are not accurately translated from the original Hebrew. Because of this, they would also contend that there were many fewer people, maybe as few as thirty thousand people in the wilderness. Unfortunately, there seems to be no clear answer although there is a great deal of research available on both sides of the issue. For a number of reasons, this latter estimate is one I feel is a better fit to the text.

Regardless of the number of people in the encampment, we know that at the center was the tabernacle. The directions God gave to Moses were exact, and He expected them to be followed exactly as He gave them. The tabernacle was part of His design for worship—how He wanted to live in relationship with His people. Exodus 25-40 includes many of the instructions God gave to create and erect the tabernacle tent, as well as each of the pieces of furniture, and the outer fence. When I refer to the tabernacle complex, I am referring to this whole area which consisted of an outer fenced courtyard with an entrance curtain on the east side and the tabernacle tent inside the outer fence.

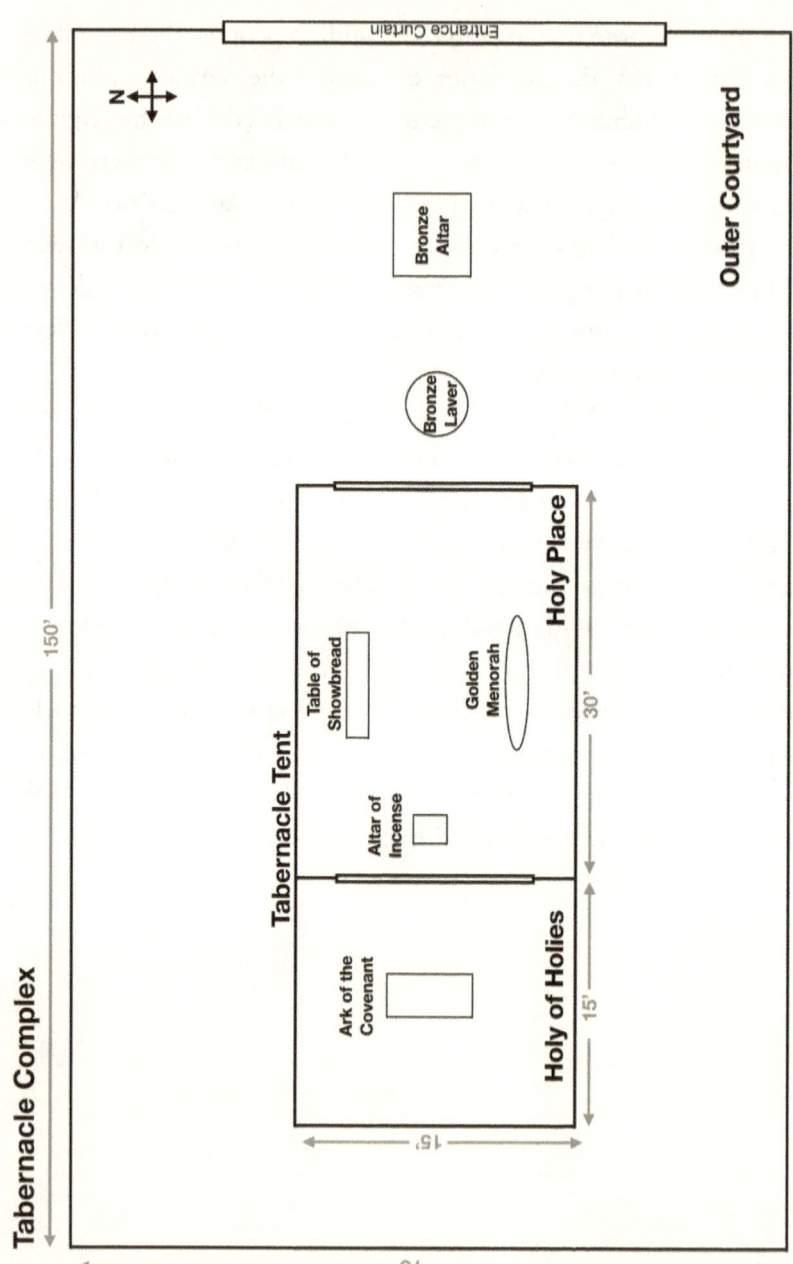

Tabernacle Complex

150'

75'

Outer Courtyard

Entrance Curtain

Bronze Altar

Bronze Laver

Tabernacle Tent

Table of Showbread

Altar of Incense

Golden Menorah

Holy Place

30'

Ark of the Covenant

Holy of Holies

15'

15'

Inside the outer fenced courtyard area was the actual tabernacle tent. The tent had two chambers—the Holy Place and the Most Holy Place or Holy of Holies—which were separated by a curtain. This tent was the heart of the camp because this is where God's manifest presence was. The bronze altar and the bronze laver also could be seen in this fenced area, and we will talk about those items in much greater detail in the following chapters.

In preparation for the work, the call was made for the people to bring forward their offerings of gold, silver, linen, precious stones, animal skins, and more. The people willingly gave. So much so, the artisans creating the tabernacle had to cry, "Enough!" They were overwhelmed with the offerings and got to a point they didn't need anymore. Once all the materials had been collected, the work could begin, and God empowered certain people with the skills needed to ensure things were made in accordance with His plan:

> Then the Lord said to Moses, "See, I have chosen Bezalel son of Uri, the son of Hur, of the tribe of Judah, and I have filled him with the Spirit of God, with wisdom, with understanding, with knowledge and with all kinds of skills—to make artistic designs for work in gold, silver and bronze, to cut and set stones, to work in wood, and to engage in all kinds of crafts. Moreover, I have appointed Oholiab son of Ahisamak, of the tribe of Dan, to help him. Also I have given ability to all the skilled workers to make everything I have commanded you. . . . They are to make them just as I commanded you." (Exodus 31:1-6, 11)

Arrangement of the Tribes of Israel

The tabernacle complex was at the center of the Israelite camp. Each of the twelve tribes were assigned to a particular location surrounding the outer fence and each had a specific role as they would march to new locations. The arrangement of this camp had order, purpose, and structure. In Numbers 2:1-3:39, we learn where each of the twelve tribes was instructed by God to camp.

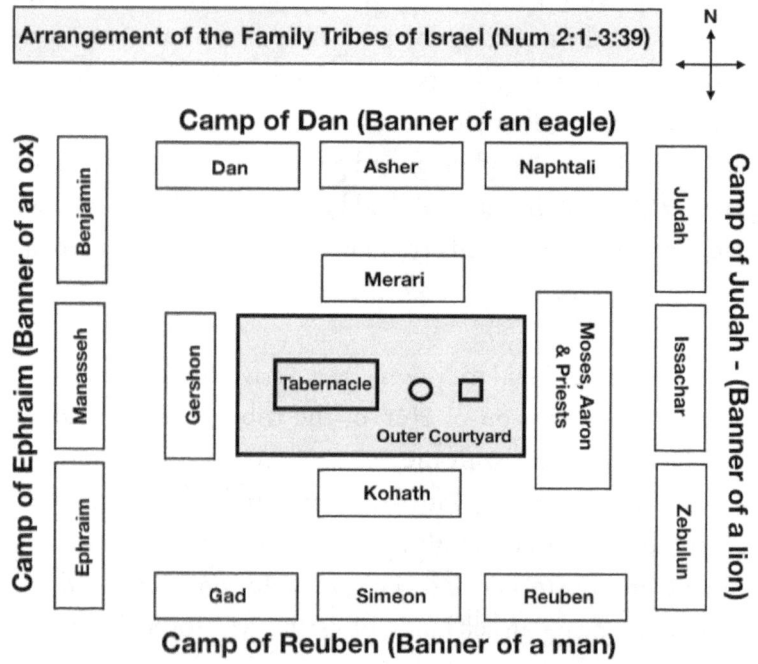

Each family group had a banner. The banner could have been raised up, so the people knew where their family group was located. The inner ring of families (those tribes closest to the outer courtyard fence), consisted of the tribes of Levi (the Levites), and then the outer ring included each of the twelve tribes. The Levites were the descendants of Levi—those who were to serve in the tabernacle as priests and musicians in service to the Lord. They were the ones to perform all the day-to-day tasks the Lord commanded regarding the tabernacle. They kept the fire on the bronze altar going, attended to the sacrifices, replaced the bread of the presence weekly, trimmed the wicks of the candles, and lit the golden lampstand each day, as well as made sure there was a continual offering of incense burning on the golden altar of incense. They were given responsibility over the tabernacle and were also the ones to care for all the sacred objects as they moved from location to location. They camped nearest the tabernacle in order to be able to accomplish these tasks when called to do so. Here is the arrangement of the tribes and their banners according to the passage listed above along with some of the responsibilities for the family groups:

- To the east of the tabernacle (under the banner of a lion):
    - o Closest to the tabernacle (inner ring) were Moses, Aaron, and the priests (sons of Aaron). Aaron and his descendants acted as the priests and high priest for Israel.
    - o In the outer ring were the tribes of Judah, Issachar, and Zebulun.
- To the south of the tabernacle (under the banner of a man):
    - o Closest to the tabernacle (inner ring) was the Kohath clan (part of the family of Levi). The Kohathites were responsible for all the holy furnishings inside the tabernacle tent (table of showbread, altar of incense, golden menorah, the

ark of the covenant, and all of the items associated with these furnishings).

    o   In the outer ring were the tribes of Reuben, Simeon, and Gad.

- To the west of the tabernacle (under the banner of an ox):

    o   Closest to the tabernacle (inner ring) was the family of Gershon (part of the family of Levi). The Gershonites were responsible for the tabernacle tent, all of the curtains for the courtyard, the tabernacle coverings, the entrance curtains for both the outer courtyard, and the tabernacle itself.

    o   In the outer ring were the tribes of Ephraim, Manasseh, and Benjamin.

- To the north of the tabernacle (under the banner of an eagle):

    o   Closest to the tabernacle (inner ring) was the Merari clan (part of the family of Levi). The Merarites were to care for all the structural elements of the tabernacle: frames, posts, bases, tent pegs, ropes, etc.

    o   In the outer ring were the tribes of Dan, Asher, and Naphtali.

Israel as a Military Camp

This camp arrangement was not uncommon in ancient times, and, in fact, it was typical of a military camp. Those who might have seen the Israelites passing through the desert would likely have viewed their camp as a war camp. The Israelites themselves probably recognized their camp was set up in a similar manner to the pagan military camps they encountered.

In a pagan military camp, there would have been an outer courtyard and a structure much like the tabernacle tent (divided into two rooms) within the courtyard. The innermost room of this tent (comparable to the Most Holy Place) would have been where the king or the pharaoh would reside and where his throne would be placed, while the outer room (comparable to the Holy Place) would have been where the king or pharaoh would meet his commanding officers—much like God met with His priests.

One of the major differences, however, was that in a pagan military camp, the king or pharaoh in his innermost room also likely had idols to the many gods that were worshiped. In Israel's camp, the people had God Himself dwelling in the Most Holy Place—not in idols made by man. In His Most Holy Place, God Himself (the King's manifest presence) would reside and the Holy Place was where the priests, who were set apart by the King for service, would come to do their duties and "minister" before the King. In this manner, the very God of the universe was on the move as a military presence with His people in the wilderness.

Most people don't think of the people wandering the desert as a military camp, but the Bible tells us the nations would tremble and were in fear at the sight of God's camp, particularly as His people came in to settle in the promised land. In the song of Moses and Miriam, we learn the pagan nations surrounding them would be in fear and trembling as God brought His people into the promised land. This was not meant to be a casual trip through the desert:

Who among the gods is like you, LORD?

Who is like you—majestic in holiness, awesome in glory, working wonders?

"You stretch out your right hand, and the earth swallows
your enemies.
In your unfailing love you will lead the people you have
redeemed.
In your strength you will guide them to your holy
dwelling.
The nations will hear and tremble; anguish will grip the
people of Philistia.
The chiefs of Edom will be terrified, the leaders of Moab
will be seized with trembling,
the people of Canaan will melt away; terror and dread
will fall on them.
By the power of your arm they will be as still as a stone—
until your people pass by, LORD, until the people you
bought pass by.
You will bring them in and plant them on the mountain
of your inheritance—
the place, LORD, you made for your dwelling,
the sanctuary, LORD, your hands established.
"The LORD reigns for ever and ever" (Exodus 15:11-18)

The God of Israel led His people to the holy promised land.
It was His desire the Israelites would conquer and displace those
set against Him. He was their commanding warrior! The people
were seen like a military war camp with God as the King and
Commanding Officer. That is most likely how the enemies of Israel
saw them. I'm not sure about you, but I never pictured a war camp
with God as the Commanding Warrior, but this is exactly how the
enemies of Israel saw the Israelites wandering the desert. When we

sing songs or hear Scripture of God as a mighty Warrior or as our King, perhaps this is the image that should come to mind.

God in the Tabernacle Complex

One of the first messages an ancient Hebrew person probably understood that we sometimes forget is that our King is a mighty warrior and there are many in His army! God set up His camp like the other military camps and His message was clear. God made it clear that He was the King of His people and His people were a part of His royal army. Israel overtook seven nations larger than itself as she entered into the promised land. Deuteronomy 7:1 explains that God would drive out and deliver their enemies into their hands. He had a part alongside Israel in the battle for the promised land. Their camp was led by a mighty and victorious warrior King and He would lead them to victory!

Elisha the prophet experienced this supernatural battle when he was in a battle against the Arameans, which seemed hopeless to his servant. When the servant of Elisha expressed his fear regarding the intimidating army they faced, Elisha said, "Don't be afraid . . . those who are with us are more than those who are with them" (2 Kings 6:16). When Elisha then prayed the eyes of his servant might see what was happening in the heavenly realm, the veil was lifted and his servant "looked and saw the hills full of horses and chariots of fire all around Elisha" (2 Kings 6:17).

The apostle Paul gives us instructions in his letter to the Ephesians to put on our own spiritual armor to stand up and do battle against the devil. Our battle not just in the world we see but in the heavenliness against evil powers as well (Eph. 6:11-12). For the most part, the battle we face is in the spiritual realm. We are taught in 1 Peter 5:8-9 that our enemy prowls like a lion looking for someone to devour.

We are not alone in the fight, though. Fear not! When the battle in your life feels fierce, God can and does send His angels to do battle on your behalf. In most churches today, we are often in tune with the softer more gentle side of Christ. He is described as the Lamb of God and often thought of as meek (or even weak) and humble. We sometimes forget He is also the God who sends out angels to do battle for us. His angels surround us and are waging war in the heavenliness on our behalf every day; we just don't have eyes to see it.

We also see Jesus clearly in the tabernacle complex. Approaching the entrance into the outer courtyard, we might recall the warning given to us that the gate to the Father is small, the road is narrow, and few will find it (Matt. 7:14). Jesus said, "I am the way and the truth and the life. No one comes to the Father except through me" (John 14:6). There is only one way to the Father both in the tabernacle and in our spiritual lives. Christ represents the narrow way to the Father and into the Holy of Holies.

The beauty is Jesus says all we need to do is to ask, and the way to the Father will be open. He says, "Ask and it will be given to you; seek and you will find; knock and the door will be opened to you" (Matt. 7:7). All we need to do is ask, seek and knock and we are free to enter in.

Foundational Elements of Worship in the Tabernacle Camp

Provision, Power, Guidance, Invitation, Holiness

As we look at the context surrounding the tabernacle, we learn of God's provision, His love, and guidance. God truly loved and wanted to be with His people. We see all through the story of the Exodus how God not only provided salvation from Egypt but also food and water to sustain the people in the wilderness. He also provided supernatural talents and all the supplies to build a dwelling place, where He could be worshiped, according to the heavenly pattern. He provided guidance as He led them as their God and as their mighty King.

We saw great strength and power demonstrated by God against Pharaoh and his people. As the camp moved through the wilderness, the surrounding nations were terrified at the sight of a camp who would have such a great King at its center. At the same time, God revealed His holiness and tender loving care as He taught His people about holiness and how to live with their creator.

Remember, the foundational elements of worship are those things that describe who God is or what He wants us to experience in relationship with Him. We experience God's provision, power, and mercy and then worship Him because of that experience. We testify about the opportunity He has given us to learn to live as people set apart from the world and as His children. We sing about His greatness. We offer prayers of thanksgiving for His mercy. We journal or write poetry about His incredible provisions in our lives. We quietly ponder the tremendous gifts He has given that we do not deserve. We worship Him in response to these things He has revealed to us.

Digging Deeper

Just like the plain linen fence surrounding the courtyard, the prophet Isaiah prophesied that Jesus "grew up before him like a tender shoot, and like a root out of dry ground. He had no beauty or majesty to attract us to him, nothing in his appearance that we should desire him" (Is. 53:2).

As priests in the kingdom of God, Christians have access through this outer "gate." The believers' access is through the acceptance of Jesus Christ as our Savior. When Jesus was preparing to leave His disciples, they were concerned because they did not know where to go or how to follow Him. Jesus told them, "I am the way and the truth and the life. No one comes to the Father except through me" (John 14:6), and then He promises the Holy Spirit to guide them in His absence. Just as the outer gate is the only way into the courtyard, Jesus Christ is the only way to God the Father. We can choose to walk past the gate or accept His invitation and enter.

1. Read Numbers 33: All the various places Israel camped in the wilderness are recorded here. What do you learn about the camp of Israel from this chapter?

2. Read Exodus 27:9-21; 38:9-20. What impressions of the outer courtyard do you have as you read these verses? What pictures come to mind?

3. Read the parable of the wedding banquet in Luke 22:1-14. What does this say to you about the invitation we have received from Christ?

Our worship response: Take some time to ponder the invitation you have received and offer up thanksgiving to God for His call on your life. Perhaps create a drawing, write a poem, or write a story of the moment Christ called you to confess and repent. Share this drawing, poem, or story with someone this week.

Prayer: Thank you, God, for calling me to be a royal priest in your kingdom. What a privilege this is! I choose to enter into your courtyard and as I walk through your pattern for worship, help me to realize the tremendous gift you have given me with this choice. Help me to live in a way that is worthy of the calling you have placed on me as one of your royal priests. Amen.

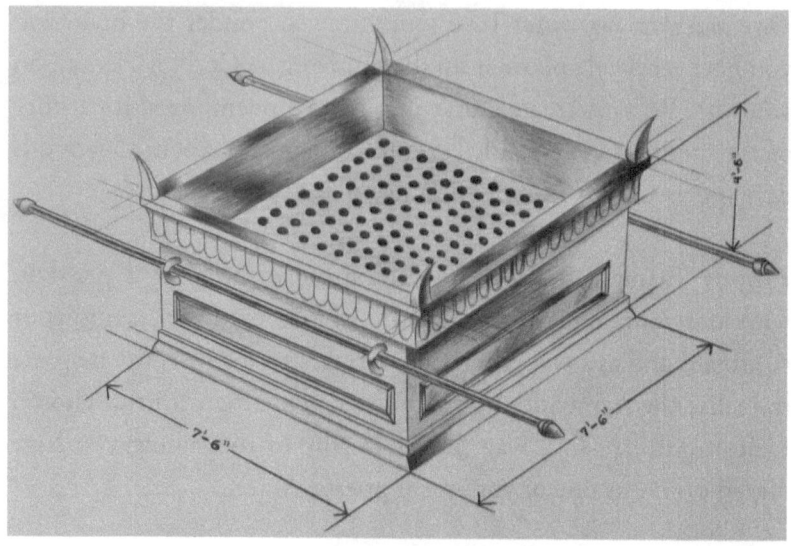

Build an altar of acacia wood, three cubits high; it is to be square, five cubits long and five cubits wide. Make a horn at each of the four corners, so that the horns and the altar are of one piece, and overlay the altar with bronze. Make all its utensils of bronze—its pots to remove the ashes, and its shovels, sprinkling bowls, meat forks and firepans. Make a grating for it, a bronze network, and make a bronze ring at each of the four corners of the network. Put it under the ledge of the altar so that it is halfway up the altar. Make poles of acacia wood for the altar and overlay them with bronze. The poles are to be inserted into the rings to they will be on two sides of the altar when it is carried. Make the altar hollow, out of boards. It is to be made just as you were shown on the mountain.

(Exodus 27:1-8)

4

Bronze Altar

The first object we experience after entering through the eastern gate of the outer courtyard is the bronze altar. The altar was a place for giving various offerings and of animal sacrifice. Although this sacrificial system is foreign to us today, the entire Jewish faith was built upon this system and thus has implications for understanding our faith today. It was also the place where substitutionary atonement was given to the Jews on a daily basis as they offered their sacrifices to God. Atonement simply means to cover over or to pacify and essentially makes a person in right standing with God again. We will discuss substitutionary atonement in a moment, but let's first take a look at the altar itself.

The altar was a box-like structure that stood four and a half feet tall and was seven and a half feet around each side. This box-like structure was made of acacia wood and was covered in bronze. It had two sets of rings attached halfway up the side so a long pole could slide through them to make it easy for carrying.

Take a moment to look around the space you are in and picture a large box in your midst that stands 4.5 feet tall and is 7.5 feet on each side. It's really not large when you consider how important it was and how often laying sacrifices at the altar is discussed in the Bible!

There are a few interesting things to note about this altar. First, the altar was made of acacia wood. If you ever have the opportunity to travel around the Sinai peninsula today, one of the things you would notice is the lack of vegetation. It is simply an extremely sparse land. Maybe at the time acacia trees were in abundance or at least readily available in the area since many of the pieces of furniture of the tabernacle were made from the wood of this tree. This type of wood has a very fine grain and is extremely durable. It is also insect resilient so it is long lasting.

A second interesting aspect of the altar was the original fire for the altar did not come from man. The new priests made animal sacrifices and placed the animals upon the altar. Then God lit the fire which consumed the offering: "Fire came out from the presence of the LORD and consumed the burnt offering and the fat portions on the altar. And when all the people saw it, they shouted for joy and fell facedown"(Lev. 9:24).

In a real sense, man made the sacrifice and offering, and God's fire consumed the sacrifice. It was the blood of the sacrifice of the animal substitute that came in contact with God's fire which allowed atonement for all God's people. This was God's holy fire, and it was meant to be continual:

The fire on the altar must be kept burning; it must not go out. Every morning the priest is to add firewood and arrange the burnt offering on the fire and burn the fat of the fellowship offerings on it. The fire must be kept burning on the altar continuously; it must not go out. (Leviticus 6:12-13)

The last interesting feature of the altar was its horns. The altar is described as having a horn placed at each corner. The Bible never seems to clearly identify the purpose of the horns, but the symbolism to the Jews was probably quite significant for a couple of reasons. First, these horns held a practical purpose—to bind the sacrifice to the altar (Ps. 118:27). Second, the horns of the altar were thought to be a place of help or refuge. In 1 Kings 1:50-51 and 2:28 we find men who in fear for various circumstances, ran to the altar and took hold of the horns as a place of refuge. When we recall the story of Abraham and Isaac we see both aspects of this symbolism at work. God spoke to Abraham and told him to take his son Isaac to the top of a mountain and offer him as a burnt offering:

Then God said, "Take your son, your only son, whom you love—Isaac—and go to the region of Moriah. Sacrifice him there as a burnt offering on a mountain I will show you. . . . When they reached the place God had told him about, Abraham built an altar there and arranged the wood on it. He bound his son Isaac and laid him on the altar, on top of the wood. Then he reached out his hand and took the knife to slay his son. (Genesis 22:2, 9-10)

As Abraham was ready to take the life of his son, an interesting event happened:

Do not lay a hand on the boy," [the angel of the Lord] said. "Do not do anything to him. Now I know that you fear God, because you have not withheld from me your son, your only son." Abraham looked up and there in a thicket he saw a ram caught by its horns. He went over and took the ram and sacrificed it as a burnt offering instead of his son. (Genesis 22:12-13)

When the angel of the Lord stopped Abraham from sacrificing Isaac, what happened? God provided a ram caught in the thicket as a substitutionary sacrifice for Isaac's life. What was the ram caught by? His horns! God secured the sacrifice in the thicket by the horns. As the animal was secured by his horns, he also offered help and a way out for Isaac, who was still laying on the altar of sacrifice. It was the ram's horns that got caught in the thicket and so the rams horns hold a great deal of symbolism to the Jews because of how God provided on Isaac's behalf.

Substitutionary Atonement

Let us dive a little further into the topic of substitutionary sacrifice. As was mentioned earlier, the entire sacrificial system was for this reason—substitutionary atonement. In the Old Testament, atonement refers to the *covering over* of sin. One life (the life of an animal sacrifice) is given for the other (the life of the worshiper). With atonement, the worshiper is granted a right status once again with God because of the sacrifice of the animal. This idea was not an invention of man. It was God who actually made the first animal substitutionary sacrifice back in the garden of Eden for Adam and Eve.

In Genesis 2, we find Adam and Eve confronted by the serpent. After they ate of the forbidden fruit, their eyes were opened, and they realized their nakedness before each other and before God. Their first response when faced with God, was to hide. God knew, of course, what they had done, and it was not long before He pronounced a curse on the man, the woman, the serpent, and the ground itself for their disobedience. God then set things right: "The Lord God made garments of skin for Adam and his wife and clothed them" (Genesis 3:21). This was the first animal sacrifice—made by God Himself. Life blood for life blood was offered. The life and blood of the animal was given so God might cover man (atone) and restore him. This example of sacrifice for substitutionary atonement began the sacrificial system in Israel and ended with the ultimate sacrifice of Jesus on the cross as the absolute substitutionary atonement for all of mankind.

Substitutionary atonement through sacrifice was not something only the Jews understood. Many people groups across the tapestry of history have made sacrifices of one form or another to their gods in order to gain their god's favor. In doing so, the worshipper has a personal involvement and can feel like they've done what is necessary to maintain their connection with their deity. As with the Israelites, food gifts of the field were brought as were animal sacrifices. Unlike the Israelites, however, it was not uncommon to also find gifts of human sacrifice offered.

The process of animal sacrifice in the Bible is extremely important because it drove the entire faith system of the Israelites. It is quite easy to imagine simply handing over an animal for the priest to deal with as payment for your sins, however, that was not at all the process. God was precise about what the process was to

entail when someone brought an offering to be burned on the altar
to make atonement for sin:

> If the offering is a burnt offering from the herd, he is
> to offer a male without defect. He must present it at
> the entrance to the Tent of Meeting so that it will be
> acceptable to the Lord. He is to lay his hand on the head
> of the burnt offering, and it will be accepted on his behalf
> to make atonement for him. He is to slaughter the young
> bull before the Lord, and then Aaron's sons the priests
> shall bring the blood and sprinkle it against the altar on
> all sides at the entrance to the Tent of meeting.
> (Leviticus 1:3-5)

It was tradition that the animal was brought by the worshiper
to the tabernacle and turned to face west toward God in the Holy
of Holies. The sacrifice was then turned to the side while the person
confessing their sin would look westward to the Holy of Holies. As
the worshiper laid their hand upon the sacrifice a prayer was spoken,
the life of the animal was taken. The individual was required to bring
the animal forward, lay his hand on the head of the animal and
slaughter it themselves. They were responsible to skin the animal
and cut it into pieces (with the exception of the Passover Lamb). It
was an extremely bloody and gruesome process and not left alone
to the priests to deal with as I have thought for most of my life.
God's people were responsible for part of the process. By laying the
hand on the head of the animal, the individual essentially passed
on his sins to the animal. Those sins require death, but the death
of the animal took the place of death of the sinful worshiper and
the substitute sacrifice was made to God to cleanse the worshiper

of their sin. The priest then collected the blood and sprinkled it on the bronze altar. The blood of the animal was shed in place of the sinner's blood and the animal's body was burned instead of the sinner's body. How amazing that God accepted the sacrifices instead for redemption and atonement. In His compassion and full of His grace and mercy He willingly chose to accept the life of the animal in place of the one who really deserved death.

Symbolism Behind the Sacrifices at the Bronze Altar

As with the tabernacle as a whole, the symbolism and order of all of the sacrifices frequently given on the bronze altar are also a reflection of our own spiritual lives. They have crossed over from being physical to being spiritual offerings that we are to still bring before God. The sacrifices that we will look at are found in Leviticus 1-7. In this passage we learn about the various sacrifices that the Israelites were commanded by God to bring before Him: the sin, guilt, burnt, grain, and fellowship offerings.

The sin and guilt offerings were those that dealt with the sin of the worshiper and were the first of the sacrifices to be given. There are some differences between the two, but a similarity is found in that they both dealt with atoning for the sin of the worshiper. The sacrifice of Jesus on the cross would be considered a sin offering. His sacrifice dealt with the sin of all mankind and offered atonement for all worshipers who follow Christ. Therefore, the sacrificial system is not dead. As a follower of Christ, our sins were ultimately atoned for by a blood offering. Jesus was the ultimate sin offering, but that doesn't mean we don't need to deal with our own sin on a day-to-day basis. We bring our spiritual sin and guilt offerings before God each time we confess our sins to Him.

Next to be offered were the burnt and grain offerings. The word for burnt offering in the Greek is *holokautōma*, from which we get our word *holocaust*. The burnt offering was to be burned in whole. The entire offering was to be burnt, representing the repentance or turning away from sin and the rededication of the entire person to God. The grain offering was also often given with the burnt offering—perhaps recognizing God's provision and a rededication of everyday life to God. Together, there is peace found in the aroma of this offering that was pleasing to the Lord (Lev. 1:9, 2:2). Likewise, in a spiritual sense, the dedication of the entire life of the worshiper to God is pleasing to Him.

Finally, the fellowship offering was given. This was given in thanksgiving for having right relationship with God. Oftentimes a fellowship offering was given as a meal offering on momentous occasions in the life of Israel. Sin was atoned for; repentance and rededication were established and fellowship or communion between God and man was enjoyed. What was one of the first things Jesus did after His sacrifice, death, and resurrection? He shared a meal with his disciples (John 21:10-14). Right standing for all mankind had been given and a fellowship offering between man and God was enjoyed.

Did you know we often follow this same pattern of sacrificial worship but in a spiritual sense? Those animal sacrifices may seem distanced and far removed, but they have simply been transferred over into the spiritual realm. We see the fulfillment of them through the lens of Jesus Christ. These sacrifices are not at all unlike our own spiritual lives. We often sin and hopefully follow with our confession of sin (sin and guilt offering). We repent and rededicate our lives to living rightly once again (burnt and grain offering). We rejoice, live in peace, and worship God as we are once again in right standing with Him (fellowship offering). Those sacrifices are a little less distant and more beautiful now aren't they?

Christ and the Altar

A fascinating exercise while reading Scripture is to place yourself somewhere in the story and allow it to engage your senses. This is a hard story to picture, but imagine yourself holding a rope tied to a perfect little animal like a lamb or a goat. You enter into the outer courtyard area, leading your animal beside you. What would it have felt like bringing that animal for sacrifice at the bronze altar? What would go through your mind as you led the noisy little animal to the priest, knowing you were leading it to a place where you would personally shed its blood? What would go through your mind as you reached out to lay a hand on the head of the animal to transfer your sin to that innocent life? How would it feel to watch its lifeblood flow out because of the foolish things you have done? How would it feel to watch the animal struggle to breathe and finally take its last breath—all because you messed up and needed to set things right with God? Not too pleasant to think about is it?

Let's take it a step further. Remove the picture of the animal you have in mind and replace your image with Jesus Christ. Picture yourself walking into the outer courtyard hand in hand with Christ. You look over at Jesus and without a word He walks with you even though you have every intention of giving Him over as your substitute sacrifice before the priest. How does it feel to see Christ in place of the animal—that substitute offering for your sin? Christ was the perfect, unblemished substitute offering killed on behalf of all mankind (Heb. 9:14). While none of us personally pounded those nails into His cross, we might as well have. It was because of our sins He had to endure death on the altar—the cross. It was our sin which caused Him to be led to be slaughtered. It was our sin that caused His blood to flow and His final breath to be taken.

It might as well have been any of us who whipped Him, pounded the nails in, and hung Him on the cross because that was what we needed—His atoning blood.

The beauty of this story is Jesus, our perfect unblemished sacrifice, went *willingly* because He knew it was for our benefit. He willingly gave His blood and His life in place of ours! He willingly endured the cross because He knew His substitutionary death (just like that animal sacrifice) made a way for heaven and earth to connect in the worshiper! It was His blood that was accepted by the Father as atonement for our sins once and for all! It was Christ's shed blood that allows our worship to be acceptable in the heavenly realms by God the Father!

> But when this priest [Jesus Christ] had offered for all time one sacrifice for sins, he sat down at the right hand of God and since that time he waits for his enemies to be made his footstool, because by one sacrifice he has made perfect forever those who are being made holy.
> (Hebrews 10:12-14)

It may surprise you to think the New Testament view of atonement and sacrifice is no different than the Old Testament. It is actually quite consistent. Just because we live under grace does not mean the law was not followed with regard to our own salvation. A blood sacrifice was still required for our atonement. No one is exempt from that fact. The sacrificial system was very much still in place at the time of Christ, otherwise His blood would have been shed in vain. Those who put their faith in Christ receive atonement through the blood shed on our behalf, not by an animal but two thousand years ago by Christ's final sacrifice, which did away with the need for daily animal sacrifices.

We may feel far removed from animal sacrifices today, but we are really not far removed at all! Christ's sacrifice was simply the final sacrifice of all daily physical sacrifices. His blood is sufficient to cover us—to atone for us—for eternity. The sacrificial system of the law was simply a shadow until it saw its complete fulfillment in Christ:

> The law is only a shadow of the good things that are coming—not the realities themselves. For this reason it can never, by the same sacrifices repeated endlessly year after year, make perfect those who draw near to worship. Otherwise, would they not have stopped being offered? For the worshipers would have been cleansed once for all, and would no longer have felt guilty for their sins. (Hebrews 10:1-2)

We see in full what the Jewish people only saw in part all of those years before Christ. In fact, it was the death of Christ that made a way for us to come into God's presence—not the resurrection. If Christ had not come and gave himself as the final sacrifice, the sacrificial system would still be in place and those ritual animal offerings would still be required for us to be in right relationship with God.

What a beautiful gift to see this portion of the law filled to the capacity—completely fulfilled! The sacrificial system is not something to fear; it is something we can be incredibly grateful for because it is still our way to God the Father. It still is quite applicable to us today. In Christ we have the ultimate and final sacrifice. Christ went to a place of abandonment and humiliation to become a sin offering for us. Just as the ropes held the animal sacrifice to the horns of the altar, the nails held Christ to the cross

to be our sacrifice. Christ died that we might live. On the altar of
the cross, a great exchange took place: His innocence for our guilt.
Peter reminds us

> "it was not with perishable things such as silver or gold that
> you were redeemed from the empty way of life handed
> down to you from your forefathers, but with the precious
> blood of Christ, a lamb without blemish or defect. He was
> chosen before the creation of the world, but was revealed
> in these last times for your sake" (1 Pet. 1:18-20).

Foundational Elements of Worship at the Bronze Altar

Mercy, Love, Sacrifice, Repentance, Forgiveness

At the bronze altar we experience God's incredible mercy. He
didn't have to create a way for us to live with Him. In our sin, we
worship or give value to things that are not God. We should each
be dead in our own sins. We selfishly chose to turn our worship
elsewhere. Through His mercy, though, God has prepared a way for
us to choose to turn back to Him. He has provided a way to repent
and be forgiven. He has provided a system through which He gives
us forgiveness for the death we should endure.

When Adam and Eve sinned by the eating of the forbidden
fruit in the garden, they forever broke their ability to have a close
personal relationship with God. God in His great mercy and
incredible love instituted the sacrificial system and made the first
sacrifice so all of mankind would have a way to be in His presence.
It was by God's hands alone that the first sacrifice was made to
literally cover Adam and Eve—first by the blood to atone for their
sins, and then by the skins to cover their nakedness.

God created the sacrificial system so we could have a close personal relationship with Him once more. The bronze altar provided the way for God's people to make continual sacrifices to keep the door open for right standing in God's sight.

In the spiritual realm and through Christ, we bring ourselves back to the altar when we fall away and confess our sin. God is faithful, loving, and merciful to meet us there and accept that sacrifice:

> For God so loved the world that he gave his one and only Son, that whoever believes in him shall not perish but have eternal life. For God did not send his Son into the world to condemn the world, but to save the world through him. (John 3:16-17)

Digging Deeper

When we accept the invitation to walk with Christ, we are called to confess and repent of our sin and accept His forgiveness. The bronze altar is the place where we discover these elements to their fullest. There is no reason at all anyone should have access to meet with the God of the universe. It is only because He offered a way for us to fellowship with Him that we have this privilege. We do this by sacrificing or confessing our sin and guilt at the cross of Christ and repenting or turning away from our sin.

Our response to the altar is to accept the sacrifice Christ made, acknowledge our sin, turn completely from it and toward God. In other words, part of our worship is also accepting God's forgiveness! It's not just about repenting and recognizing God forgives, it's about actually accepting forgiveness and not trying to carry the weight of guilt and shame with us into the Most Holy Place. Oftentimes, we tend to hold ourselves in contempt far more than God does. Once we confess, we need to embrace God's forgiveness and the truth about who we then become: God's children—holy and dearly loved (Eph. 5:1).

While the more formal, liturgical churches pause at the bronze altar and corporately confess and repent of their sins, unfortunately, the altar is a place many churches seem to jump over during their corporate worship service, except perhaps when they choose to do communion. Most churches are often great at welcoming people into God's presence, but then proceed to try to lead people directly into the Holy of Holies without pausing to experience God through a time of corporate confession, repentance, and acknowledgement of forgiveness. If we are honest with ourselves and with each other, we often don't walk into church having taken the time to confess, repent, be cleansed on our own. If our leaders in the churches don't lead us this way, it is up to us as believers and lovers of God to take matters into our own hands to come prepared to our corporate services. We are God's priests and maybe we need to take on this responsibility ourselves. When was the last time you took time before a worship service to confess your sins to Him?

1. Read Exodus 27:1-8 and 38:1-7. Describe the burnt offering in your own words.

2. Read through Leviticus 16. What do you learn about the Day of Atonement? How does this passage inform you about the life of Christ? What are some of the parallels with the life of Christ?

3. Read Hebrews 9 and 10. How is Christ both our High
    Priest and the sacrifice offered by a high priest on the Day of
    Atonement?

Our worship response: In Acts we see Peter telling the Israelites
what they must to do be saved. He says, "Repent, then, and turn to
God, so that your sins may be wiped out, that times of refreshing
may come from the Lord" (Acts 3:19). Take a moment and seek
what God may be asking you to lay on the altar today. Light a
candle to represent your offering to Him, for Him to do with as
He pleases.

How do you prepare to go into a corporate worship service?
Are there some intentional actions you think about or that you do?
If not, what might you consider doing next time? Take those steps
before going into your next corporate worship service.

Prayer: I admit I don't always get things right God but thank you
for the cross of your Son! Jesus, thank you for the price you paid on
the cross, so I can be in right standing before You. Forgive me for
those things that keep me distant. Allow me to be covered with the
blood of Christ, so I might be made holy once again. Holy Spirit,
prompt my heart and mind when I begin to go astray and lead me
back to the altar where I can give the offering of my confession and
receive forgiveness once again. Amen.

Then the LORD said to Moses, "Make a bronze basin, with its bronze stand, for washing. Place it between the tent of meeting and the altar, and put water in it. Aaron and his sons are to wash their hands and feet with water from it. Whenever they enter the tent of meeting, they shall wash with water so that they will not die. Also, when they approach the altar to minister by presenting a food offering to the LORD, they shall wash their hands and feet so that they will not die. This is to be a lasting ordinance for Aaron and his descendants for the generations to come."

(Exodus 30:17-21)

They made the bronze basin and its bronze stand from the mirrors of the women who served at the entrance to the tent of meeting.

(Exodus 38:8)

5

Bronze Laver

The next item in the journey toward the Most Holy Place is the bronze laver. The laver was simply a basin that was used to wash from after the sacrifices were offered. It is here we really begin to experience differing levels of holiness with each step we take toward the Most Holy Place. The nearer we move to God in the Most Holy Place, the more holy the space becomes. For example, the courtyard is considered a more holy place than the camp surrounding the courtyard. Likewise, the Holy Place within the tabernacle is more holy than the outer courtyard, and the Holy of Holies is considered the most holy place in the camp. God radiates holiness and so as we move closer to Him, the more holiness we experience around us. When the priests were consecrated (dedicated) into service for the Lord, they had to go through a process by which they would come into a state of holiness. Doing this allowed them to come near to the Lord without fear of death. Cleansing at the bronze laver was an important step in this process toward holiness.

There are actually a lot of unknowns with regard to the bronze laver. There are no clear descriptions in the Bible of what the laver may have looked like, but as Exodus 38 suggests, it seems to have been composed of two pieces: the basin and its stand. Whether they were joined together as one piece or not is not known. Regardless, God commanded that the laver be placed between the altar and the tabernacle tent and that Aaron and his sons (the Levitical priests) were to wash both their hands and their feet before entering the tabernacle. God also commanded that if the priests did not follow His words, they would die (Exodus 30:20-21).

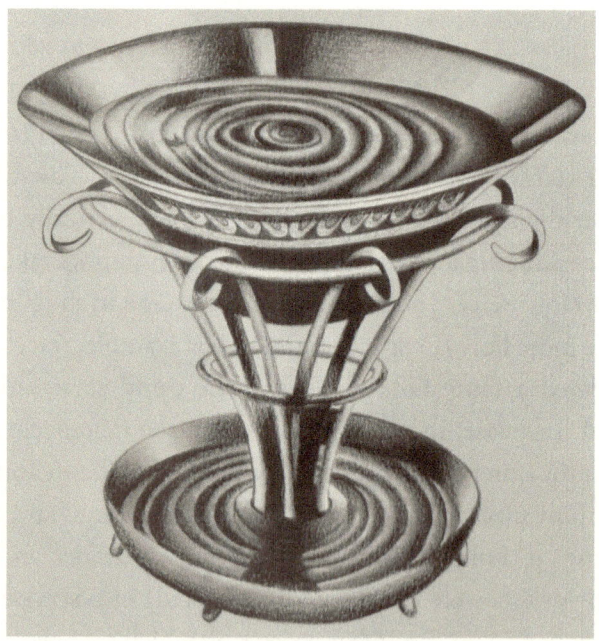

The Bible is similarly unclear as to how a priest might wash both his hands and feet from the laver. Some artist renditions portray a basin placed on a stand with a separate bowl or cup which might be used to dip in the basin to help wash the priest's feet. Other artists renderings (like the one above) suggest that the stand also included a basin at ground level. This essentially was a laver with a double basin: one on top to cleanse the hands and one below to cleanse the feet. While the design of the second one might make it easier for the priest, the first one probably fits a little more closely with the description in the Bible since the Bible makes no mention of a second basin that must be filled with water.

The one thing that is quite clear from the text, however, is that the laver was crafted of bronze and mirrors (Ex. 38:8). These mirrors were not like those we have today but were more likely a highly polished piece of metal (see Job 37:18). Why do you think God called for it to be made out of mirrors? Why not simply unpolished bronze? What was the purpose of using mirrors? Perhaps it was a visual reminder for the priests of the necessity of washing away the dirt and grime of their lives in order to enter into God's presence? It may have merely been a way for the priest to see their own reflection and be reminded of their humanity and need for God. Scripture never indicates why God commanded it to be made using mirrors. We can only speculate.

The main point of the bronze laver was simple: cleansing, purity, and holiness. Holiness is of utmost importance to God because He is holy. Over and over again in Scripture, God commands His people to be holy (e.g., Leviticus 11:45, 19:2, and 20:26). A search in the NIV translation of the Bible pulls up at least eighty-five instances of the exact phrase "be holy." Holiness is a big deal to God! Even Aaron, the high priest, was commanded to wear a turban with a golden plate attached with the words "Holy to the Lord" engraved on it when coming before God in the Most Holy

Place (Ex. 28:36). It is not hard to imagine that a priest who raises this turban to his head must recognize the seriousness of living up to those words and being holy and clean before God.

What Does It Mean to Be Holy?

So let's look a little closer at holiness. To be holy is simply to be set apart for God's use and His purposes. The spiritual journey of a believer has many parts to it that are related to holiness, including justification, sanctification, and glorification. At the same time, we can refer to our holiness in a positional sense or in a practical sense. To experience all of these, is to experience a journey through the varying stages of holiness. Sometimes these terms are thrown around in Christian circles while some are left without really understanding what they mean. Each term has to do with holiness and a progression from one state of holiness to another.

Positional Holiness

Positional holiness refers to our standing in the heavenlies before God. At the moment of our conversion (or our justification), we become positionally holy before God. Our position with God is that we have been covered by the blood of Christ and we have been cleansed and made holy for God's purpose. This position does not change with time, and, in fact, nothing can change this position with God. We were cleansed by the blood of Christ once and for all when we made the decision to follow Him alone (Heb. 10:10). We were made holy. If our lives on earth would end at this moment, and we were to meet God face to face as Christ followers, we would be in the position of being seen as holy because of the blood of Christ shed for us.

Justification

As mentioned above, our positional holiness came as a result of our conversion. Justification is often the term used to describe the conversion or change in a person's life from being an unbeliever to becoming a believer in Christ. It is the point in time within which the unbeliever comes to faith and is declared to be "not guilty" by God because of the work of Jesus Christ. They were first declared unholy as an unbeliever and then transitioned to holy at the point of their justification. In a legal sense, to become justified is to give a reasonable explanation for something otherwise unlawful. Paul makes it clear in Romans 6:23 that we should die because of our sin and not have access to God. Through Christ, however, our sinful nature is still present, but we are exempt from suffering the penalty of our sin. The death of Christ has justified us or made us righteous before God.

The apostle Paul puts it this way:
> Therefore, since we have been justified through faith, we have peace with God through our Lord Jesus Christ, through whom we have gained access by faith into this grace in which we now stand. And we boast in the hope of the glory of God.
> (Romans 5:1-2)

Sanctification

Justification is the first step in the process of sanctification. The believer's life is justified before God and the journey toward becoming more Christlike begins. While justification happens as a one-time event, sanctification is a lifelong process. It is the process of becoming more holy (set apart) than you once were. Hopefully, throughout our lives, we will become more Christlike and live in a manner that is more holy than when we first met Christ. It is part of our job as Christ followers to strive to live a life following Christ's example. As Scripture instructs:

> "You were taught, with regard to your former way of life, to put off your old self, which is being corrupted by its deceitful desires; to be made new in the attitude of your minds; and to put on the new self, created to be like God in true righteousness and holiness." (Ephesians 4:22-24)

Practical Holiness

Sanctification is the ongoing process and practical holiness refers to our state of holiness at any given moment in time. We live in a sinful world and still succumb to sin on a daily basis. Quite frankly, there are many times we are not living holy lives. Practical holiness is something that changes depending on how we are living at the moment. There are times when we are not living for God and choosing instead to live for our own desires. There are times unwholesome talk comes from our mouths or unhealthy thoughts are rehearsed in our minds. There are times when we hurt others with our actions or with our speech. These are the times when we are not living as holy unto God—practically speaking. These are the times when we need to repent and come back into proper communion with God.

Glorification

When we speak of God's glory, we refer to his magnificent beauty. In the eternal realm, Christians will be made glorious after death as they live eternally with Him. This refers to the state of glorification. Paul teaches us that as followers of Christ, we are being changed with "ever-increasing glory" (2 Cor. 3:18). One day our sanctification process will be complete, and we will be glorified with Christ! It is the completion or the complete fulfillment of our salvation. Glorification refers to the end result of our sanctification journey and is experienced after our lives are over, and we stand in the presence of God.

Holiness and the Levitical Priests

This sanctification process (moving from justification to glorification) is incredibly important. God created a way for mankind to be cleansed and made holy on a daily basis. He laid down extremely clear instruction on how the Israelites were to worship Him and how they were to be made holy. In fact, God gave an entire book (Leviticus) of instruction to the Levitical priests, so they might know how to become holy to minister in the tabernacle.

The modern-day reader often struggles with Leviticus because it seems so detached from our way of life and includes instructions that no longer seem valid. During the time of the sacrificial system, however, Leviticus was vital in the daily worship of the Levitical priests. They were to obey the instructions perfectly. Doing so was of utmost importance toward being cleansed and made holy before God. Many of these instructions actually have spiritual principles today that are completely valid if we study them.

Obedience to God's instruction was vital to these priests. Their lives depended on it. Obedience to God's instruction is obviously still valid today. We are not exempt! We are still required to bring spiritual sacrifices and set ourselves apart as holy to the Lord. As

New Testament believers, it's easy to disassociate ourselves from the Old Testament, thinking we live under grace and no longer live under the law so the sacrificial system no longer applies. Our understanding of holiness, sacrifice, or sanctification may look a little different than it did during the time of the ancient sacrificial system, because our understanding of holiness has moved from the physical to the spiritual realm, but holiness is still important.

There are days many of us miss the mark when it comes to living a holy lifestyle. We may find ourselves focused on the wrong things or doing things simply for our own gratification instead of seeking God's desires. We've all been there. This is partly why this study of the tabernacle is so enlightening. God laid out a blueprint for living out this practical holiness in our lives on a day to day basis. The process of repentance, forgiveness, cleansing, and holiness is in the plan we see laid out in the ministry of the tabernacle. It teaches us that the way of access to God is through sacrifice and the way to holiness is through separation from sin. This was just as valid for the Levitical priests as it is for us today as we are now a part of God's royal priesthood!

Christ and the Laver

While the purpose of the laver has some beautiful symbolism attached to it regarding our position with God, the water used in the laver is just as rich in symbolism. It was imperative the priests washed with water before they were allowed to enter the tabernacle tent. Water represented cleansing and purification and was a necessary part of the sanctification process. In other words, the washing with water was often a symbol of being purified or cleansed of the defilement and sin, thus it allowed the worshiper to be brought to a more holy state.

David used this imagery regarding water in the Psalms: "Wash away all my iniquity and cleanse me from my sin. . . . Cleanse me with hyssop, and I will be clean; wash me, and I will be whiter than snow" (Ps. 51:2, 7). The author of Hebrews also speaks of being able to boldly go into the Holy Place because we have been washed with water: "And since we have a great priest over the house of God, let us draw near to God with a sincere heart in full assurance that faith brings, having our hearts sprinkled to cleanse us from a guilty conscience and having our bodies washed with pure water" (Heb. 10:21-22).

Paul addressed the Corinthians and noted that many of them were believers who had previously lived sinful lives as fornicators, adulterers, thieves, covetous, drunkards, and swindlers. Paul told them that regardless of their past, they would inherit the kingdom of God because *they were washed*, sanctified, and justified in the name of Jesus Christ by the Spirit (1 Cor. 6:9-11).

When you think of being washed with water in a spiritual sense, the image of baptism may come to mind. It should! Have you ever considered that your baptism was symbolically portrayed over three thousand years ago in the wilderness with the exiled Israelites? Cleansing with water at the laver was not something only for Old Testament times. It was not just to wash off the blood of the animal sacrifices. Cleansing at the laver was a foreshadowing of the cleansing, renewal, and rebirth we experience by the Spirit of God at our baptism. As the priests ritually washed the blood of the sacrifices off their hands, they were made clean and holy— able to go into the tabernacle to minister before the Lord. At our baptism, we make a visual proclamation before others that we have confessed and repented of our sins (at the bronze altar) and are now considered a new creature in God, cleansed and forgiven. That is the ministry of the bronze laver.

Baptism of Jesus and the Consecration of Aaron

Let us also take a brief look at the baptism of Jesus and the bronze laver. In Matthew we read that Jesus came before John to be baptized. He speaks these words regarding His own baptism: *"Let it be so now; it is proper for us to do this to fulfill all righteousness" (Matt. 3:15).* Just after His baptism, the Holy Spirit of God descended, and Father God declared this was His Son. We see the entire trinity of God here in Jesus' baptism.

What did Jesus mean that this should be done to fulfill all righteousness? First, let's look at the life of John the Baptist. John the Baptist's father, Zechariah, was from the line of Levi, the same tribe Moses, Aaron, and his sons came from. The succession of high priests through the generations would eventually find Zechariah in the mix of names. Zechariah was not only a priest in the temple, he was of the lineage of the high priestly family. Does this matter with regard to John baptizing Jesus? Jesus was not being baptized as part of a repentance from sin, which John seemed to be baptizing for, so why was He baptized? There are some scholars who link the baptism of Christ with the consecration of Aaron and his sons who ministered as high priest. Let's look a little closer at the consecration of the priests to see the connection.

In Leviticus 8:5-9:24 we see the consecration ceremony and induction of Aaron as the high priest of God's people. In this passage, Moses brought Aaron and his sons forward, *washed them with water* and then clothed them with the priestly clothes. He then took the anointing oil (often symbolic of the Holy Sprit) and anointed Aaron's head with the oil. After all the remaining sacrifices and rituals were performed, Aaron and Moses went before God. In response, the glory of God was seen by all the people and God's fire came and consumed the burnt offering that had been placed on the altar. The people witnessed this and fell down in worship. Aaron had been consecrated as high priest, seen the glory of God and affirmed by God's fire.

Consecration of Aaron	Baptism of Jesus
Moses brought Aaron and his sons forward and washed them with water.	John the Baptist (of the line Aaron) baptized Jesus. It was to be done for all righteousness (to be morally right or justifiable), unlike our own baptism.
Moses anointed Aaron's head with the anointing oil.	The Holy Spirit (like the anointing oil) came down and rested on Jesus.
Moses presented Aaron, and the glory of God appeared, validating his priesthood.	God the Father spoke from heaven in the hearing of all the witnesses. Jesus is the chosen One—God's Son.
God consumed the sacrifice given, thereby accepting Aaron as the high priest of His people.	Jesus was compared with the Lamb of God the very next day by John (John 1:35-36). Jesus was the sacrificial lamb that eventually was placed on the altar as an offering.

It is interesting to consider the parallels between these two stories. There are some who believe that the washing of water at the baptism of Jesus was really a consecration for His ministry on earth and ultimately as our High Priest. This means that there was a passing on of the role from one high priestly line (John the Baptist) to another (Jesus Christ).

So we know holiness is important to God. How often do we pause and reflect on our own lives and seek to wash away the dirt and grime before we enter into worship with our holy God—whether corporately or personally? Our baptism was a one-time event of cleansing, purification, and testimony, but do we consider this same aspect of washing on a daily basis before God?

The priests were faced with this ritual every single day as they ministered before the Lord. They were reminded every day of their need to be holy before God. It was their job to follow God's specific directions in order to be holy before God. As part of His New Testament believing royal priesthood, we were certainly washed clean of guilt and sin when we professed Jesus as our Savior, but because practically we still sin, we still need to confess our sin. For those ancient priests they had a daily reminder built into their schedule by God. What is your daily reminder?

> *"If we confess our sins, He is faithful and just to forgive us our sins and purify us from all unrighteousness."*
> (1 John 1:9)

Foundational Elements of Worship at the Bronze Laver

Holiness, Purification, Sanctification, Baptism

Purification and sanctification go hand in hand with holiness simply because they are part of the process that leads to holiness.

Again and again throughout the ministry in the tabernacle, holiness is at the center and the heart of the ministry that happened there. We are purified at the moment of salvation, but just because we are cleansed and purified of our sin once, we can't assume we are always in right standing with God in the practical sense. We are not always living holy lives, and practically speaking, sometimes we are downright unholy. We live in this tension of being holy yet not completely holy all the time.

Consider what living in this tension might have been like for Aaron as the high priest of God's people. He probably had to do some serious mental gymnastics as he served in the role he did, and I think many pastors and worship leaders in our church today can identify with Aaron. He regularly put on all the priestly garments and topped it off with a "crown" etched with the words "*Holy to the Lord.*" He, and he alone, then entered into God's presence once a year on behalf of all his people. He was the only one of the thousands of God's people who had the privilege to meet with God one on one.

Do you think he ever felt proud and thought things, such as: "I am in the most unique position among all these other people I live with. I am in a higher up position before God than those people who aren't allowed into the tabernacle. Look at me going into a place where no one else is allowed. God thinks I'm pretty special!" Or perhaps he suffered with thoughts of a lowly position: "I should not be allowed to do such ministry before God. The people see only my outward sin. If they knew the thoughts in my head, they would see why I should be completely disqualified from ministering before the Lord like I do. I don't deserve to be here."

Many people in leadership in God's church today probably have moments when they think too highly of themselves and other times when they think too lowly. The thing is, it doesn't matter what our thoughts are, it matters what God thinks of who we are. Put yourself in the shoes of a pastor or a worship leader—both visible roles in the church. How would you feel if every time you went before your congregation, the leaders of the church required you to put on a ball cap that has the message "I am holy to the Lord" printed on it? How would it make you feel to be the only one asked to wear such a bold message? How do you think the rest of the congregation would feel? Would you feel like they were putting you up on a pedestal as being more holy than they are because of your position? Would you feel a little awkward or uncomfortable being set apart from all the other people in your church? How would you respond to the leaders in your church asking you to do such a thing? Take it a step further. Would you wear such a cap in public outside of church? In your grocery store? In the hardware store? In your community?

It might be a little uncomfortable to imagine and yet, is this not the message we should *all* be wearing? This is our testimony! This is what and who we are. We are a righteous people, holy, and set apart for God. We already wear this mark of holiness on us each and every day; in our hearts as beloved children of God. Do we let that message, a message declaring we really are holy people, shine out? Remember, we have been justified! Remember, we are being sanctified each and every day! Remember, we are to be set apart from the world as the objects of God's holiness to serve as witnesses to God's work on earth. We are His ambassadors to the world around us. This is how God views us, and how we need to think of ourselves—a holy people, set apart from the world for God and as His witnesses to those who do not yet know him. This is the privilege of a priestly role—and that is who you are!

Digging Deeper

At the beginning of the early Christian church, Peter preached to the crowds of people who had gathered around him. He gave a passionate sermon about how Jesus was the Messiah they had all been waiting for and that this same Jesus had also been put to death by them. When the people realized this, they were grieved and asked, " 'Brothers, what shall we do?' And Peter said to them, "Repent and be baptized, every one of you, in the name of Jesus Christ for the forgiveness of your sins, and you will receive the gift of the Holy Spirit' " (Acts 2:36-38).

This short passage demonstrates the tabernacle pattern up to this point: invitation, confession, repentance, forgiveness, and cleansing. God met with them, and they responded with an action—to repent and be baptized. As a result, three thousand people came to faith on that one day! It was both a moment of their being made holy and righteous before God and also a beginning point of their sanctification process.

In Christ we have received the ultimate cleansing from our sin. Christ is able to wash us clean of our sin, and we no longer need to carry it around. In Ezekiel 36:25-27 God spoke to the Israelites saying, "I will sprinkle clean water on you, and you will be clean; I will cleanse you from all your impurities and from all your idols. I will give you a new heart and put a new spirit in you; I will remove from you your heart of stone and give you a heart of flesh. And I will put my Spirit in you and move you to follow my decrees and be careful to keep my laws." These words are for us too! As a priest would wash his hands and feet before coming into the presence of God, we also can be cleansed from the corruption of the world.

1. Read 2 Chronicles 4:2-6 and 1 Kings 7:23-40. How does this bronze laver of the Jerusalem temple compare with the bronze laver of the tabernacle in Exodus 30:17-21?

2. Read Exodus 29:1-9. This describes the process for consecrating (making holy) the priests of the Levites. Consider Jesus' baptism in Matthew 3:13-17. What did Jesus mean by "it is proper for us to do this to fulfill all righteousness"? Is there a connection between the consecration of the priests and the baptism of Jesus?

Our worship response: Take some time to draw near to God and be cleansed by Him. Turn on some reflective music and picture yourself standing in a waterfall. Let go of all the things you have asked forgiveness for. Let Him wash those things away. When you seek His forgiveness, He will pour out His forgiveness and purification on you. Receive His forgiveness and let the promise of the everlasting life he has given you refresh and revive your parched spirit.

Prayer: "Have mercy on me, O God, according to your unfailing love; according to your great compassion blot out my transgressions. Wash away all my iniquity and cleanse me from my sin" (Ps. 51:1-2). "Cleanse me with hyssop, and I will be clean; wash me, and I will be whiter than snow" (Ps. 51:7). What joy there is in being washed clean of sin and shame and being at peace with You once again, God! Thank You for Your cleansing! Amen.

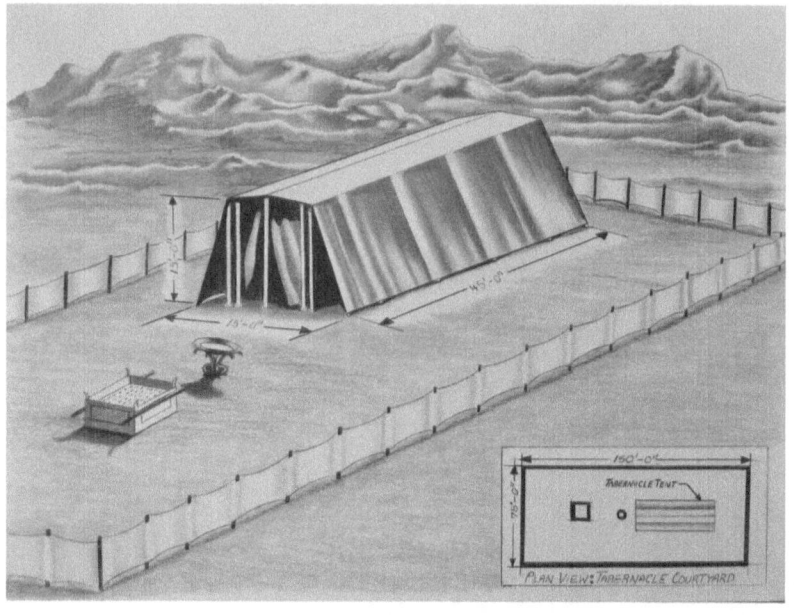

The Lord said to Moses, "Tell the Israelites to bring me an offering. You are to receive the offering for me from everyone whose heart prompts them to give.

(Exodus 25:1-2)

"Then have them make a sanctuary for me, and I will dwell among them. Make this tabernacle and all its furnishings exactly like the pattern I will show you.

(Exodus 25: 9)

6

The Tabernacle Tent

*W*here would most people say the most sacred or holy place on earth is? What comes to mind when you picture that place? What does it look like? How does it sound? Is it stunning? Is it breathtaking? Peaceful perhaps? I'm guessing there are a fair percentage of people around the globe who might picture the Vatican in Italy, perhaps in Jerusalem, or even at the Dome of the Rock. Many others may say that place is in their local church or simply being in nature alone with the Creator. The spectrum is broad. There are many amazing cathedrals and beautiful holy places around the world, but in the Old Testament the most holy place on earth was inside a tent. Was it stunning? Absolutely! It was covered in gold. Breathtaking? Well, if you did not approach and enter properly, your breath could very literally be taken away—for good!

Once the sacrifices were offered and the cleansing ritual finished, the priests could then enter into the tabernacle tent without fear of being struck dead. The outer court saw man dealing with his sin and guilt and moving him to holiness. The inner court (inside the tabernacle tent) was a place where the priests would commune with God and the other priests as they ministered before the Lord.

As we begin to map out what this tent looked like, keep in mind the average Israelite never had the opportunity to view the holy things inside the tabernacle. They had the opportunity to hear all about them from their description in the Scriptures or from stories told by the priests, but the beauty of all the gold pieces was enjoyed by the priests alone. Only the Levitical priests from the line of Aaron were permitted in the Holy Place.

Exodus 26 and 36 give a description of the tabernacle tent and how it was constructed. It was housed inside the outer courtyard fenced area and was approximately forty-five feet long by fifteen feet wide and fifteen feet high. It was made of a wooden frame structure covered by four layers of linens and animal skins. There is no specific indication as to how it may have looked from the outside, whether or not it had a pitched or flat roof, but tradition seems to indicate it was more likely a flat roofed tent.

The detailed framework of the tabernacle tent was created of acacia wood covered in gold and held together by rings of solid gold and poles covered in gold. The north, south, and western walls of the tabernacle were constructed of this golden frame-like structure while the eastern "wall" of the Holy Place and the Most Holy Place was covered with a linen curtain or veil so the priests could move inward from the eastern end of the tent. The appearance of the walls from the inside was likely similar to a latticed wall and not a solid wall simply because an acacia tree on the Sinai peninsula would not grow large enough to create planks wide enough for a solid wall. Each piece of this wooden frame was covered in gold and was held upright at its base with a tenon which would fit into a mortice or base of silver. From this latticed framework, the inner layer of linens was draped and you would have been able to see this layer through the golden lattice.

Layers of the Tent

This first layer of fabric in the interior of the tent was made of finely twisted linen woven of blue, purple, and scarlet thread and embroidered with images of cherubim (Ex. 26:1). Cherubim were often thought of as the guardians of God (Ez. 28:14) and so it is not surprising they were used inside the tent. The Egyptians were gifted in the weaving of linens and certainly the Hebrew women also picked up some of these skills. Interestingly, these beautifully hand-crafted curtains were seen only by the priests. There is a spiritual principle here that we will come back to in a moment.

The next layer of the tent was made of woven goat hair fabric that was either black or dark in color. There is actually a reference to the dark tents of the nomadic people in Song of Solomon 1:5. In this passage, the bride asks not to be judged for her dark complexion, likely derived from a nomadic lifestyle. She compares her dark complexion to the black-hair tents of Kedar, one of the sons and nomadic tribes of Ishmael. These black goat-haired tents were not uncommon in these ancient times. The goat hair fabric was carefully stitched together and laid over a layer of brightly colored curtains. The goat-haired layer was weather resistant and slightly longer than the colored first layer. If for some reason this layer were to have gotten wet, the goat hair fibers would swell creating a weather tight tent. For this reason, and a few others, the dark bedouin tents are still used in the Middle East today.

There is much more detail on the crafting of the first and second layers of the tent as compared with the third and fourth layers. We know from Scripture, the third layer was made with ram skins dyed red and the fourth layer with another durable leather. What this durable leather was is up for debate. Some say it was made of either badger or antelope skins. Other translations refer to this leather being made of sea cows or even dolphins. Interestingly, there is a sea creature similar to the manatee called the dugong dugong that is native to the Red Sea and Gulf of Aqaba whose skin could fit this description. In the end, we never really know what it was made of, however, we can probably assume both the third and fourth layer of the tent were made with similar dimensions to the second layer because it would have had to have been laid over the second layer. We have nothing definitive in Scripture about the size or shape of these outer two layers.

Inside the Holy Place

Inside, the tent there were two rooms divided by a curtain or veil. This is the curtain that protected the Holy of Holies. The Holy Place, or the tent of meeting (Lev. 16:17), was the larger of the two chambers or rooms and was thirty feet long by fifteen feet both in width and height. At 450 square feet, it was about the size of a small studio apartment today. The temple of Jerusalem came later as a permanent replacement for the tabernacle and was larger in size than the tabernacle tent, but its purpose and layout remained the same. In fact, the temple veil torn in two at the death of Christ (Luke 23:45; Mark 15:38) was the veil dividing the two rooms.

Tabernacle Tent

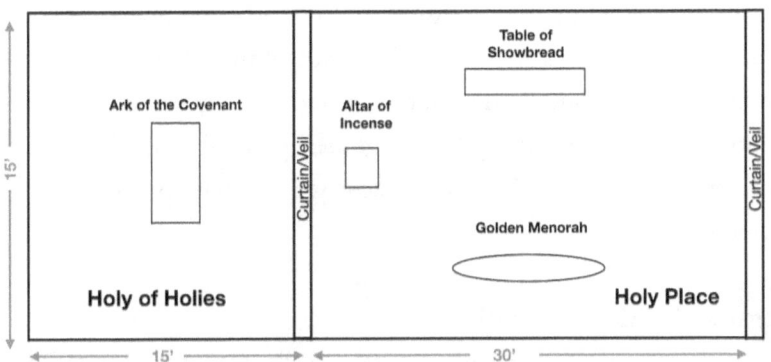

The common Jewish person would have been allowed in the outer courtyard, but the Holy Place was the chamber that separated God from the common person. Only the priests were allowed inside. They were to act as the representatives of the people to God and as the ambassadors of God to the people. Interestingly, we still see some of this type of architecture in our churches today. You often have an outer lobby area (outer courtyard) through which you then enter the sanctuary (Holy Place). Often, all focus is directed toward the front of the church where you might see an altar or a pulpit (Most Holy Place) and the place where many of the more sacred events happen, such as baptism, communion, preaching or speaking the Word of God.

Upon entering the Holy Place, the first thing you would notice is all of the gold. Even our most elaborate cathedrals today pale in comparison to the beauty that would have been found inside the tabernacle! While bronze and silver were the primary metals used for the outer courtyard and the foundation bases of the tent, gold was the main metal used for the objects inside the tabernacle itself. All the furniture, various implements (dishes, cups, wick trimmers, trays, censers), and even the frame of the room were all created from or covered in gold. Remember, one ton of gold was collected to create the objects and adorn the inside of the tabernacle! Picture everything in your living room covered with gold. Imagine the entire Holy Place shining by the golden glow of candlelight from the golden menorah. You can almost see the majesty and glory of God on display.

Inside the Most Holy Place

The second room of the tabernacle was entered by first walking through the Holy Place. This inner sanctum was where God dwelled. While all the Levitical priests were permitted into the Holy Place, only the one priest designated as the high priest was permitted to enter this part of the tent and then only once a year on Yom Kippur (Day of Atonement). This innermost room is referred to as the Most Holy Place, the Holy of Holies, or even the Sacred of Sacreds. It was considered to be the most holy of all holy places and the most sacred of all sacred places on earth. It was the place where God's Shekinah glory was found. It was where His manifest presence was found on earth.

The Most Holy Place was also the space set aside to house the ark of the covenant—the footstool of the throne of God. The room itself was a perfect cube (fifteen by fifteen by fifteen feet) and might be comparable to an average sized living room. At first, this may not seem to be significant, but there is actually tremendous symbolism found in the dimensions of this room! The only other space in the Bible described as a cube is the New Jerusalem. In Revelation we read:

The angel who talked with me had a measuring rod of gold to measure the city, its gates and its walls. The city was laid out like a square, as long as it was wide. He measured the city with the rod and found it to be 12,000 stadia in length, and as wide and high as it is long. (Revelation 21:15-16)

The city described here is fourteen hundred miles long, wide, and high; it is a cube just like the Holy of Holies. In the New Jerusalem, it will be as if we are living in the Holy of Holies with God!

Once the Israelites were in the promised land, *"Solomon began to build the temple of the Lord in Jerusalem on Mount Moriah, where the Lord had appeared to his father David"* (2 Chron. 3:1). After the temple was built in Jerusalem the tabernacle was no longer necessary. King Solomon was the one who built the temple in Jerusalem on the space known as the Temple Mount, which currently houses the Muslim Dome of the Rock. This is the place on which the temple stood for hundreds of years until it was destroyed in AD 70. What's interesting is the place on which the Temple Mount is located is thought by many scholars to be the same Mount Moriah where Abraham was asked by God to sacrifice his son Isaac: *"Then God said, 'Take your son, your only son, whom you love—Isaac—and go to the region of Moriah. Sacrifice him there as a burnt offering on a mountain I will show you"* (Gen. 22:2).

Tradition says the rock currently inside the Dome of the Rock is the same place where Abraham was to sacrifice Isaac. At the same time, the Muslims believe this is the same rock from which Muhammad ascended. In speaking of the holiest place on earth, this is perhaps one of the most uncontested sites. Nowhere else on earth is one small plot of land so special, so holy, and so coveted.

The Other Dwelling Places of God

There is an interesting literary device used over and over again in Scripture called a chiasm or an inverted parallelism. It is a literary structure composed of comparisons in reverse order. I bring this up here, because it is an interesting way to also view all of the dwelling places of God from Genesis to Revelation. In doing this, we also see how consistent and creative God is.

Having been a musician for most of my life, the best way I can describe a chiasm is to think of the song "Twinkle, Twinkle, Little Star." If I were to write the lyrics in the form of a chiasm it would look like this:

> A: Twinkle, twinkle, little star, how I wonder what you are!
> > B: Up above the world so high, like a diamond in the sky.
> A: Twinkle, twinkle, little star, how I wonder what you are!

If you were to hum the tune, you would also find the first line and the last line of music sound exactly the same. We have one musical phrase (*A*), a contrasting musical phrase (*B*), and then a duplicate of the first musical phrase (*A*). The A-B-A structure is found both musically and with the text. This same idea is found in Scripture. Here is how it works using Mark 2:27 as an example:

> A: The Sabbath was made
> > B: for man,
> > B′: not man

A′: for the Sabbath

This verse is probably familiar to you. As you look at the structure, you will see *A* is related to *A′* as they both refer to the sabbath. Likewise, both *B* and *B′* are related to one another as they both refer to mankind. Both sets are not quite identical, but they are related. That is why the second time the letter is listed it includes the tick mark.

Here is another example from Scripture. In 1 John 1:6-7 we see the inclusion of a climax statement:

A: If we claim to have fellowship with him
    B: and yet walk in the darkness,
        C: we lie and do not live out the truth.
    B′: But if we *walk in the* light, as he is in the light,
A′: *we have fellowship* with one another, and the blood of Jesus, his Son, purifies us from all sin.

In this example, *A* corresponds to *A′* and *B* corresponds to *B′*. This time, however, we have a climax found in *C*. It is unlike anything before or anything after it. "We lie and do not live out the truth" is the focal point of this passage.

Now let's apply this to the dwelling places of God, and you will see how creative God is! Here is how the dwelling places of God might be mapped out. God dwelt:

A: ...in the garden temple of the garden of Eden
    B: ...in the mobile tabernacle in the wilderness
        C: ...in the fixed temple in Jerusalem
            D: ...in the flesh as the person of Jesus Christ!

C´: …in the Christ followers in Jerusalem

B´: …in mobile Christ followers reaching to the ends
of the earth

A´: …in the garden temple of the New Jerusalem

In Genesis, God told Adam and Eve to be fruitful and multiply to the ends of the earth (Gen. 1:28). It seems His original desire was to dwell with us and see His kingdom expand to the ends of the earth. Similarly, Jesus' last words to the disciples were to go to all the nations on earth, baptize them, and teach them to obey all He commanded (Matt. 28:16-20). The mission has not changed! God still desires to dwell with all His people on earth.

We now live in *B´*, which finds its parallel in the tabernacle. The tabernacle and all of the foundational elements there not only are a shadow of heaven, but they apply in the spiritual realm to us today. We have the opportunity to see the partial spiritual fulfillment of all the tabernacle was designed to be. How amazing is our God! He gives us order and structure in the Scriptures to live by and then models this same structure in the ordering of where He chooses to dwell!

Foundational Elements of Worship in the Tabernacle

Remembrance, Beauty, Splendor, Majesty

There are many instances of God remembering His people and then acting in response. God remembered Noah and made the flood waters recede (Gen. 8:1). He heard the groaning of His people in Egypt and remembered His covenant with Abraham. He looked on them and was concerned (Ex. 2:24-25). He remembered His love for Israel and all the nations saw salvation as a result

(Ps. 98:3). Jesus instituted the new covenant during the last supper and asked His disciples to remember His broken body and His shed blood as they took the bread and the wine (Luke 22:19-20).

There are times when God does something so special He commands His people to do something to remember. When the Israelites were saved out of Egypt and led into the wilderness, God commanded them to remember what He did for them by celebrating Passover every year (Ex. 12:1-14). Likewise, when the people crossed the Jordan River into the promised land, God commanded them to build an altar of stones in remembrance for what He had done for them and to stand as a witness to any who might pass by. (Deut. 27:1-8).

To this day, we celebrate communion as an act of worship and in remembrance of Jesus. He commanded that whenever we come together to break the bread and take the wine, we do it in remembrance of His sacrifice for us (1 Cor. 11:23-26). How seriously do we take those times of communion? Do we actually think of them in terms of an altar of remembrance? That is what they are. God doesn't need to be reminded. We do!

Even the tabernacle was designed in such a way to ensure the people of Israel would remember God. He designed it so we can see the spiritual application now even though the physical tabernacle has passed away. Believe it or not, we can even see Christ and His ministry for us in each of the layers of the tabernacle tent!

As has already been mentioned, the inner most layer of the tent was where all the beauty was. There was literally a ton of gold and intricate fine craftsmanship in the linens and the furniture as well as the accompanying implements. All the beauty and splendor of God was experienced by Aaron and his sons as God's high priests. The average Israelite only saw the outer layer, which had none of this beauty.

Isaiah 53:2 tells us Jesus "had no beauty or majesty to attract us to him, nothing in his appearance that we should desire him." The beauty was inside our Savior! Only those who could peer in and see who Jesus truly was could see the beauty inside. As believers living under the new covenant of Christ, we have all of the beauty and splendor of the Lord within us. We are the living tabernacle of God. He dwells in us with all His majesty and glory. Think about that. The beauty only the high priest could experience then now lives in each of us. What a tremendous blessing! A blessing that should lead us to remembrance and to respond in worship.

The next three layers help us to remember the ministry and person of Jesus. The second layer of goat hair reminds us of the story of the scapegoat. Once a year, on the Day of Atonement, the high priest would place his hands on the head of the scapegoat and transfer all the sins of the people onto the animal. The animal was then released into the wilderness (and probably led over a cliff or killed in some manner not recorded) to carry those sins with it. Jesus was like the scapegoat carrying our sins away.

It is interesting that the next layer of ram skins was dyed red. Remember the ram caught in the thicket in the story of Abraham and the sacrifice of Isaac? That ram was the atoning sacrifice just as Jesus is our atoning sacrifice! Perhaps the skins were dyed red to link the blood of the atoning sacrifice with the animal skin. It seems that God built spiritual applications into every last detail of His house that He desires we remember.

Lastly, while we are not quite certain what the outer layer was made of, it seems that it was not very impressive. Had it been, we probably would have much greater detail about it. The outermost layer of the tent and the part the common person would see as it rose above the outer courtyard fence was unimpressive. There was really nothing to draw the person there except for the fact that they probably heard the stories of the amazing beauty inside this tent. This brings us back to the passage in Isaiah 53. The verse above tells us there was nothing that would attract us to Jesus other than what was inside of him. He was probably similar in appearance to any other common Israelite. For the person who only looks on the outside, they would not notice His beauty. Only those who strive to see Jesus for who He really was see the beauty inside the tent of His fleshly being.

The tabernacle is perhaps the most creative visual representation of the holiness of God! Every piece of furniture and implement tells a story and can lead us to understand Christ better. Every action commanded there has a spiritual principle that can guide us into an understanding of who we are in relation to this holy God whom we serve. He has crafted this visual image for us to connect with Him, and He is so worthy of all of our worship!

Digging Deeper

My husband and I enjoy backpacking in the summer. We load up everything we need to get us through a few days and head for the mountains. One of the things that is a necessity for us is our tent—our mobile dwelling place. We can hike around all day long, but our tent is our place of rest and safety (although any bears or mountain lions might think differently). At the end of the day we have a shelter to protect us from the sun or the rain. There is comfort knowing that we have a place to "belong" even in the wilderness.

I wonder what it was like for the Israelites to know that God was dwelling in their midst. Consider the following words of the psalmist:

How lovely is your dwelling place, LORD Almighty!
My soul yearns, even faints, for the courts of the LORD;
My heart and flesh cry out for the living God.
Even the sparrow has found a home, and the swallow a
nest for herself, where she may have her young— a place
near your altar, Lord Almighty, my King and my God.
Blessed are those who dwell in your house; they are ever
praising you. (Psalm 84:1-4)

As God's physical dwelling place on earth now, we can
experience that same sense of security and peace in our lives here
on earth. Point to ponder!

1. Read through all of Psalm 84. The psalmist was referring to the
    temple—the dwelling place of God at that time. Place yourself
    in the psalmist's shoes. What insight do you gain from this
    passage that you might not have seen before?

2. John 1 speaks of Jesus coming to this world to "dwell" or
    "tabernacle" with us. Do a little research into the Feast of
    Tabernacles (See Leviticus 23:33-44 and John 7). This feast
    was a celebration and remembrance of God dwelling with the
    Israelites in the wilderness. What connections do you find
    between this feast and the life of Jesus?

Our worship response: Take some time to really ponder the idea of *being* the dwelling place of God. Perhaps even grab your tent this weekend and ponder this in the wilderness. Ask Him to show you what that means for you. It's a huge responsibility and an incredible blessing. Take a walk or get out into nature. Enjoy the beauty of God's creation, knowing that one day we will be in a garden temple once again. Perhaps take a sketch pad and draw a place of beauty that you find or snap some pictures and add your favorite Bible passage using a photo editing app and make it a background on your phone or computer.

Prayer: Thank you for the wonderful gift of your presence in my life. What an honor to be considered a dwelling place for You! You didn't have to choose to dwell within me. But I am so humbled and grateful that You did! In all my messiness and even with my struggle with sin, You still chose me as a place to dwell. Help me to live worthy of that calling. Help me to take You to the ends of the earth as best I can and share this marvelous gift I've been given with others. Amen.

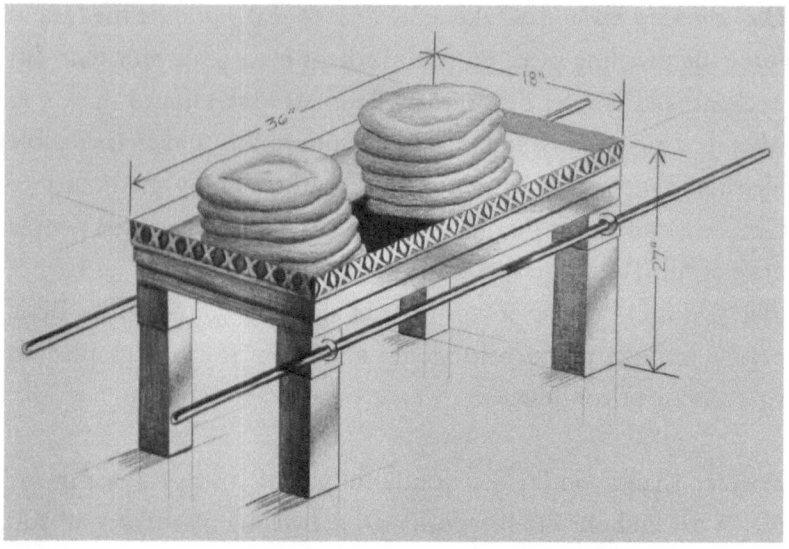

Make a table of acacia wood—two cubits long, a cubit wide and a cubit and a half high. Overlay it with pure gold and make a gold molding around it. Also make around it a rim a handbreadth wide and put a gold molding on the rim. Make four gold rings for the table and fasten them to the four corners, where the four legs are. The rings are to be close to the rim to hold the poles used in carrying the table. Make the poles of acacia wood, overlay them with gold and carry the table with them. And make its plates and dishes of pure gold, as well as its pitchers and bowls for the pouring out of offerings. Put the bread of the Presence on this table to be before me at all times.

(Exodus 25:23-30)

7

Table of Showbread

The first item for study in the Holy Place is the table of showbread. As you entered through the eastern curtain of the tabernacle tent, the table would be found on the right hand or north side. If you stop and picture the dimensions of this table, you would realize how small it really was. It was approximately thirty-six inches long by eighteen inches wide by twenty-seven inches high. Like the bronze altar, its main structure was made of acacia wood, but the entire piece was covered in gold. It had a beautiful gold molding around the top edge of the table and four gold rings (one at each corner) through which poles covered in gold would have been inserted to lift and transport the table without touching it. Exodus 25:29 and Numbers 4:7 explain that there were also dishes, pitchers of wine, and bowls of pure gold on the table with the bread.

The purpose of the table was to hold twelve loaves of unleavened bread representing the twelve tribes of Israel before God. This bread was a visible demonstration to the priests of the covenant God made with His people who were also always in His presence (Lev. 24:8). The bread on this table had many different names all referring to the same thing: showbread, bread of the presence, shewbread, and bread of the face. These loaves were to be always before the Lord in the tabernacle, always in His presence or before His face. At the end of each week on the Sabbath, the bread was removed, distributed, eaten, and replaced by the priests in the holy place. It is assumed the bread remained fresh and did not become stale because its nearness to God made it holy.

Christ and the Table

When you stop to consider the bread and wine placed on the table of showbread, it's not difficult to picture this as a foreshadowing of what we know today as the communion service. The priests broke bread before God and distributed it to one another on behalf of the twelve tribes of Israel. They also poured out the wine as drink offerings at this table. It was here that they were in communion with God and with each other.

If we look a little deeper, we see symbolic meaning in the process of making both the bread and the wine as well. First, the wine for the drink offering was created by the *crushing* of grapes that then went through a fermenting process. Next, the bread was made of freshly harvested grain *crushed* and made into flour. Leaven, or yeast, symbolized sin and since these loaves of bread were made for the holy place, it is likely the bread for the table was unleavened although Scripture does not say specifically one way or another. When baking bread, there are natural bacteria found in the dough which may cause it to puff up and appear to rise. However, during the baking process for unleavened bread, the dough is often *pierced* and *striped* to reduce any rising from these natural bacteria. It ends up having an appearance similar to a saltine cracker with small holes in it.

Considering both of these things, Isaiah 53:5 tells us Jesus "was *pierced* for our transgressions, he was *crushed* for our iniquities; the punishment that brought us peace was upon him, and by his wounds *[stripes]* we are healed" (emphasis added). Just as the grain and the grapes were crushed, pierced, and striped, Jesus' body was crushed, pierced, and striped for us. Next time you take the communion elements, realize God has given you a visual representation of what actually happened to Christ to hold in your hands.

The Last Supper

Jesus said, "I am the bread of life. Whoever comes to me will never go hungry, and whoever believes in me will never be thirsty" (John 6:35). He is the bread and the way of fellowship with God the Father. At communion, Jesus took the unleavened bread, broke it and said, "This is my body given for you; do this in remembrance of me" (Luke 22:19). Just as the bread was broken in the holy place as a reminder of the old covenant with God, Jesus broke the bread as a reminder of His new covenant with us (Jeremiah 31:31-33).

The last supper celebration Jesus had with His disciples was in the context of the yearly Passover Seder meal celebrated by the Jews (Matt. 26:17; Mark 14:12; Luke 22:7-8). The Passover meal begins the weeklong Festival of Unleavened Bread, a time to remember to remove sin and be set apart for God. To this day, the Seder continues to be celebrated yearly as a meal of remembrance because it connects us to an event in history when the Jews placed the blood on their doorposts to escape the last plague of Egypt—death of the firstborn.

The final plague had come upon Pharaoh and all of Egypt. The Jews were not exempt from this one. Exodus 12:29-30 tells us the Lord God came during the night and took the life of all the firstborn, both man and animal alike. Those who heeded God's warning and placed the blood of a sacrificed lamb on the door were the only ones spared. After the last plague, God gave salvation to His people. They escaped Egypt to live in the wilderness with Him, worshipping Him as His covenant people.

We know it was during this celebration meal in the final day of His life that Jesus instituted communion and called us to remember His sacrifice. Do you realize though, Jesus showed the disciples how He came as the fulfillment of this traditional meal? The disciples saw how Jesus' life fit all of the elements of the Passover Seder story: the unleavened bread, the sacrificial lamb, the drink offering poured out. It's all tied together in Jesus!

When Jesus instituted communion, He took the salvation story and showed us how we are connected to those ancient covenant people. Gentiles are now also a part of His covenant people! As Gentiles, we can also share in the Seder meal and rejoice as we see Christ fulfilled throughout the story.

Foundational Elements of Worship at the Table

Communion, Fellowship

At the table of showbread, we experience both communion and fellowship as foundational elements of our worship. When the priests took care of the weekly duties at this table, we see God built a weekly time of communion into their schedule. The breaking of bread was done with the other priests at the table and before the presence of God—hence the name, bread of the presence. In many churches today, Communion, or the Eucharist, often takes the form of something quite personal and introspective—looking back on the death of Christ. This was not the manner in which Communion was done in the first century church.

The term *Eucharist* literally means thanksgiving. In the early church, giving thanks to God was a part of Communion. The Didache (pronounced did-ah-kay) was an early first century document that sheds light as to how the community of believers celebrated their lives together as brothers and sisters in Christ. The instructions given in this early church document for Communion include celebrating together with a meal and with thanksgiving. Yes, we can be introspective and, yes, it is good to recall the incredible sacrifice Jesus made on our behalf, but it is not inappropriate to rejoice and be thankful in a Communion service as well.

Digging Deeper

It takes many months to bring a loaf of bread into being—from the planting of the seed, to the harvesting of the grain, to the grinding of the grain, and all the way to baking the bread. Similarly, wine does not happen overnight. It takes a great deal of time to grow the grapes, harvest and crush the grapes, ferment the juice and then to allow it time to come to its fullness. In our busyness and fast-food world, we sometimes lose the satisfaction that comes from fellowshipping around a table as we eat.

One of the last things Jesus did with His disciples before His death and one of the things He made sure to do with His disciples after His resurrection was to share a meal. When we share a meal with one another, we share in each other's lives. We create memories when we take the time to connect with one another. To commune with others is simply to share and exchange thoughts, ideas, and feelings, particularly on a spiritual level, and that's what happened between Jesus and His disciples during their resurrection breakfast. I'm sure it was a meal full of questions, recollection, and probably laughter and joy too.

My husband suggested we start a tradition a few years ago that we call Luddite Night. A Luddite was a person from the age of the industrial revolution who was against the technologies coming out during that time. For us it represents putting away the phones, iPads, computers, and TV and enjoying an evening of stories, laughter, games, and pondering Scripture together with friends and family. The idea came when the power went out one evening during a summer thunderstorm. As we sat around in the candlelight, it dawned on me: "This is so beautiful and peaceful. Why don't we do this more often?"

On Luddite Night we invite family members and friends over to share with us. We put away the gadgets, light up the candles, share a meal (usually finger foods of some sort which don't require cooking), and play games or discuss some thought-provoking topic. The kids particularly like this because they get to be in on the discussion and have quality time with the adults in their lives. We always come away refreshed.

It is easy to let the busyness of life take over and miss the joy that comes from fellowshipping around a table with our family and friends. When we stop to take the time to enjoy fellowship with our loved ones, we come away with a deeper connection to each other. So it is with God. When we don't take the time to fellowship with God (through Scripture, song, and recalling His work in our lives) life may begin to consume us, and we can become spiritually hungry and thirsty. Oh the joy that comes when we take the time to be filled by Christ! It is so satisfying.

1. Read carefully through the following scriptures: John 6:35;
    6:51-58; Luke 22:19-20; 24:30-32. Place yourself in the story.
    Describe in detail what this may have been like to experience.

2. If you have never been to a Passover Seder before, do a little
    research about it. What are some of the symbols used during
    the Seder meal? How does it impact your understanding of the
    Last Supper?

Our worship response: Take some time to have fellowship and
break bread with God and others as the priests did in the Holy
Place. Create your own Luddite Night. Turn off the lights, light
some candles, pull out some snacks, and then have everyone place
a question they have about the Bible or about God in a hat. Take
turns drawing out a question and then discuss it together. You
might be surprised by the conversations you can have.

Prayer: Time with You can be so sweet, God. Help me to spend
more time with You. Forgive me for often placing things ahead of
You that aren't important. Holy Spirit, prompt my heart to slow
down and not be so consumed by the busyness of life. Scripture
tells me to look for wisdom as if searching for a hidden treasure
(Prov. 2:1-5). As I take time in sweet communion with You,
God, please help me find those beautiful treasures of wisdom and
understanding. Amen.

Make a lampstand of pure gold. Hammer out its base and shaft, and make its flowerlike cups, buds and blossoms of one piece with them. Six branches are to extend from the sides of the lampstand—three on one side and three on the other. Three cups shaped like almond flowers with buds and blossoms are to be on one branch, three on the next branch, and the same for all six branches extending from the lampstand. And on the lamp stand there are to be four cups shaped like almond flowers with buds and blossoms. One bud shall be under the first pair of branches extending from the lampstand, a second bud under the second pair and a third bud under the third pair—six branches in all. The buds and branches shall all be of one piece with the lampstand, hammered out of pure gold. Then make its seven lamps and set them up on it so that they light the space in front of it. Its wick trimmers and trays are to be of pure gold. A talent of pure gold is to be used for the lampstand and all these accessories. See that you make them according to the pattern shown you on the mountain.

(Exodus 25: 31-40)

8

Golden Menorah

―――――

*I*n the tabernacle the golden lampstand or menorah stood to the left or south side of the Holy Place. There are no specifics about the size of the menorah, but what is known is actually pretty detailed. It is clear from Scripture that it was made of one solid piece of gold weighing approximately seventy-five pounds. The cost for materials in today's dollars would be well over $1.2 million for this one item. The main shaft had six branches extending from it and each branch held a number of cups shaped like buds and almond flowers. Seven lamps were placed upon it which would burn a clear virtually smokeless olive oil in order to keep the Holy Place well lit. These lamps were kept burning from evening until morning.

Notice all the different elements that make up the menorah: a central shaft, branches, buds, flowers. All of these were made from one solid piece of gold. What might this resemble? It is actually a great description of a tree. But, you might ask, "What difference does this make?" This is where things get really fascinating.

The tabernacle, as we know, was God's special dwelling place during the wilderness wanderings of the Israelites. He designed the purposes of each element the tabernacle contained, but there was an earlier dwelling place where God made Himself manifest to man—the garden of Eden.

Garden of Eden

The garden of Eden is actually thought by most scholars to be the first temple—a garden temple—and the prototype for all future temples. God must have loved the beauty of the garden because He used many of the elements found in the garden of Eden as design features of the tabernacle and later the temple. The last temple or dwelling place of God is also in the form of a garden and is found at the end of the Bible in Revelation 21 and 22 as the New Jerusalem. If you read through Genesis 2-3 and Revelation 21-22, you will see some significant similarities. I have highlighted these in the chart on the following page.

There are a couple of items I'd like to touch on a little more in depth. The first is with regard to Adam and the priests. Adam's purpose in the garden of Eden was to cultivate it and to keep it (Gen. 2:15). In the original Hebrew it is to *awbad (serve)* and to *shawmar (guard)*. *Awbad* is to be a servant or in bondage to, although not necessarily with a negative connotation. When this word is used with regard to service to the Lord, it is used with a more positive connotation, like serving with joy or delight. *Shawmar* means to guard or protect as with a hedge of thorns. The pairing of these two words is not found very often in the Bible. Interestingly though, one of the few places they are used together is also with regard to the service and ministry of the priests in the tabernacle. In other words, Adam was the first priest of God's garden temple.

Garden Temples Compared with the Tabernacle/Temple

Garden of Eden	Tabernacle/Temple	New Jerusalem
On a mountain (Ezek. 28:14, 16)	On a mountain (Exod. 15:17)	On a mountain (Ezek. 43:12; Micah 4:1-2; Rev. 21:10)
God's presence was there (Gen. 3:8)	God's presence was there: The same verb for "walking back and forth" in the garden (Gen. 3:8) is the same as describing God's presence in the tabernacle. (Lev. 26:12; Deut. 23:14; 2 Sam. 7:6-7)	God's presence is there (Rev. 21:3)
Tree of life and knowledge of good and evil (Gen. 2:9)	Lampstand in the holy place resembling a tree (Exod. 25:31-40)	The Lamb is the lamp (Rev. 21:23); tree of life (Rev. 22:2)
Water – rivers (Gen 2:10)	Bronze laver—cleansing water	Water (Rev. 22:1)
Gold and precious stones (Gen. 2:11-12; Ezek. 28:13)	Gold and precious stones	Gold and precious stones (Rev. 21:11; 19-21)
First sacrifice for sin offered by God	Sacrifices at bronze altar by God's people	No sacrifices needed!
Food in the garden provided for Adam (Gen. 2:9)	Sacrifices and bread of the presence provided food for the priests	Trees bearing fruit crops (Rev. 22:2)
Center of the garden represented the Holy of Holies	Holy of Holies described as a cube	New Jerusalem described as a cube (Rev. 21:16)
Adam as the first priest (Gen. 2:15)	Levites served as God's priests	Priesthood of all believers
Guardian cherubim (Gen. 3:24)	Guardian cherubim in the decorations and on top of the ark of the covenant	Ark of the covenant (Rev. 11:19)

The second item to note is with regard to the atoning sacrifice made after the fall. It was God who provided the first atoning sacrifice for sin and thus initiated the whole sacrificial system. God took the skin of an animal(s) to provide the clothing to *cover* Adam and Eve's nakedness (Gen. 3:21). Remember, to atone for something means to *cover* over; it is no longer seen. The first blood sacrifice by God became a literal covering placed on Adam and Eve. As part of the priestly guardian role, Adam was to keep out anything unclean. He failed in this task, and God took the first steps of the sacrificial system to make right what went wrong.

Christ and the Menorah

As we have been looking at Christ in comparison with all the various elements so far, the lampstand most easily seems to represent both the life of Christ and our own lives. Jesus spoke of Himself saying, "I am the light of the world. Whoever follows me will never walk in darkness, but will have the light of life" (John 8:12). However in Matthew 5, He calls us the light of the world: "You are the light of the world. . . . In the same way, let your light shine before men, that they may see your good deeds and glorify your Father in heaven" (Matt. 5:14, 16).

In the lampstand, we see something uniquely special about the life of a believer and Christ. Paul says in Galatians "I have been crucified with Christ and I no longer live, but Christ lives in me" (Gal. 2:20) It is Christ in us that makes us the light of the world. Sometimes it may seem hard to remember we are called children of the light. I've often struggled with depression and the darkness can be so consuming at times, but I love Paul's encouragement:

For you were once darkness, but now you are light in the Lord. Live as children of light (for the fruit of the light consists in all goodness, righteousness and truth) and find out what pleases the Lord."
(Ephesians 5:8-10)

There are three key things here to focus on. The first is the phrase *"But now you are light in the Lord."* You live in a dark world, and you may be experiencing times of darkness, but because Christ lives in you, you are *already* light. Satan may try to have you believe darkness lives in you, but it simply isn't true. If you live with Christ as your Lord and Savior, no matter how dark a place you feel you are in, rest in this promise that you *are* light in the Lord, even if you don't feel that way. Your place may seem exceptionally dark, but Christ still dwells in you and His light is also within you. Persevere!

Second, we are told to *"live as children of the light."* We are to choose to live with our focus on Christ so our light will burn brightly. We all make bad decisions from time to time, and if you feel your light is shining dimly, turn your focus on Christ and stand firm in the promise that you are already light. Seek then to make good decisions which will lead to goodness, righteousness, and truth. Step by step, you will get there again and the light of Christ already in you will shine brightly.

Lastly, what pleases the Lord? Jesus commanded us to go and take His light and spread it to the ends of the earth. "Therefore go and make disciples of all nations, baptizing them in the name of the Father and of the Son and of the Holy Spirit, and teaching them to obey everything I have commanded you" (Matt. 28:19-20).

Foundational Elements of Worship at the Menorah

Mission

When you read through the description of the lampstand, you may have been awed by the beautiful object it must have been—pure gold artistry, shimmering by the light of the lamps. That beautiful image is the light of Christ which now lives in us! The golden menorah serves as a reminder to us to be on mission for Christ and to seek to expand His kingdom here on earth by taking the light of Christ into the world around us. That is our worship response. We have experienced the beauty we know of as the light of Christ and need to take the light into an extremely dark world that desperately needs it. Jesus commissioned us as His ambassadors when He said, *"Go into all the world and preach the gospel to all creation"* (Mark 16:15).

Digging Deeper

We already understand Jesus is the light of the world and that He calls us to be a light to the world as well. However, there is another aspect of the lampstand not discussed above. In Revelation 1 and 2, John receives a vision from the Lord. In this vision, he sees someone who is thought to be Christ, moving among seven golden lampstands while holding seven stars in His hand. Each of the stars represent an angel connected with one of the churches, which are portrayed as lampstands (Rev. 1:20). In these chapters, Christ speaks to each angel regarding their church and the witness the church holds in their communities. In other words, He addresses the light each church shines within their communities.

There is obviously a personal stake in letting our light shine for the world, but have you thought about the communal aspect?

Have you ever paused to consider the light that shines from your church into your community? What is the reputation of your church in the community where you live? Does your church stand true to the commands of God? Do they compromise so they can be relevant? Is your church persecuted yet stands firm for Christ?

We are not silo's for Christ in this world; we are part of a community. If we light one candle in a black room, we have enough light to get by. If we light several candles in a dark room, the darkness has no chance! We are stronger for Christ together than we are separated. What can you do to be a part of your church and strengthen its light in the dark world we live in?

1. Take a moment to read John 1:1-18. Ask the Holy Spirit to help you see this passage with fresh eyes. What does it mean to you to be a child of the light? Other Scriptures to consider: Psalm 27:1; Matthew 4:16; 5:14; John 3:19-21, 8:12, 9:5.

2. Read Ephesians 5:8. Are you a light in the darkness around you? If so, how are you specifically being a light for God? What steps can you take to shine brighter? If you feel like you are not shining as a light before God, what is one thing you can change today to shine brighter for God? Use that as your first step and take it in boldness in the next twenty-four hours.

Then add another step. Journal your thoughts as to why you hesitate to allow Christ to shine brighter in your life.

3.   Read Revelation 1 and 2. Make a list of the things Christ says to each church. Where do you see your church in these lists? What are the strengths of your church? What are its weaknesses? In what ways can the light you shine strengthen your church? In other words, what are the strengths you bring that can help strengthen your church?

Our worship response: Choose an evening to gather your community of friends and loved ones together. Begin with one lit candle and read 1 John 1:7. Let the next person light a candle to add to the first and read 1 Corinthians 1:10. Let the next person light a candle to add to the first two and read 1 Thessalonians 5:14. Continue to add candles and read the following passages: Galatians 6:2; Proverbs 27:17; Romans 12:16; John 15:12-13; Hebrews 10:24-25; 1 Peter 2:9-10; Ecclesiastes 4:9-12; Ephesians 4:4-6. Notice how much better you can see with each additional candle. End by reading Philippians 2:3-16 and close your time in prayer thanking God for the light of His Son.

Prayer: Lord, to be a light in the darkness is a big responsibility. It brings hope to those who have no hope and comfort to those who have no comfort. Light brings clarity where there may be feelings of chaos. Help me to live boldly and shine brightly for You! While the light reflected from me can do positive things for those who seek it, it also makes me stand out for persecution from those who don't. Help me keep my candle shining brightly regardless of the circumstances I find myself in. Amen.

Make an altar of acacia wood for burning incense. It is to be square, a cubit long and a cubit wide, and two cubits high—its horns of one piece with it. Overlay the top and all the sides and the horns with pure gold, and make a gold molding around it. Make two gold rings for the altar below the molding—two on opposite sides—to hold the poles used to carry it. Make the poles of acacia wood and overlay them with gold. Put the altar in front of the curtain that is before the ark of the Testimony—before the atonement cover that is over the Testimony—where I will meet with you.

(Exodus 30:1-6)

9

Altar of Incense

The final object in the Holy Place is the altar of incense. The altar of incense was also made of acacia wood like many of the previous items and overlaid in gold. It was eighteen inches by eighteen inches by thirty-six inches tall and as you entered the Holy Place, this altar would be directly ahead and resting just before the veil to the Most Holy Place. Like the table of showbread, there was also a gold molding around the top edge and golden rings attached for the gold covered wooden poles to slide through for transportation. Similar to the bronze altar, it also had four horns, one at each corner. However, this altar was used primarily to burn incense.

Exodus 30:34-38 describes the various components used in equal proportion that make up the incense used on the altar. This was a special blend to only be used for God (to be set aside as holy for Him) and not to be used simply for pleasure. There were five ingredients present: gum resin (thought to be the sap from a balsam tree), onycha (most often understood as either matter from a sea creature or a flowering plant), galbanum (a Persian plant which readily grows in the Middle East), and frankincense or (resin from the Boswellia tree). In addition to the spices, salt was also added.

Salt is a common substance but held great significance in ancient Israel for social and economic purposes. It was used in trade and the sharing of it became a symbol of friendship. There are a number of different reasons salt is mentioned in the Bible. It was used as a symbol of purity, life, and everlasting covenant. It was used in preservation, and even represented death, if overused. Leviticus 2:13 gives the instructions to season all of the offerings with salt—the salt of the covenant of God. Most scholars seem to view the presence of salt in the incense mixture with regard to its purity or as the symbol of the everlasting covenant between God and His people.

The purposes of burning incense are also many. Incense may have been used simply to mask the odors from the extensive animal sacrifice that took place. Its fragrance is also described as a pleasing aroma ascending to God in heaven. In addition, the high priest was to burn incense on the Day of Atonement and to take it into the Holy of Holies so the smoke could shield the atonement cover and spare his life. Symbolically, the rising smoke was also associated with prayer (Ps. 141:2; Luke 1:9–10; Rev. 5:8; 8:3–4).

Unlike the bronze altar, blood was applied to the altar of incense only once each year on the day of Yom Kippur or the Day of Atonement:

> Aaron must burn fragrant incense on the altar every morning when he tends the lamps. He must burn incense again when he lights the lamps at twilight so incense will

burn regularly before the LORD for the generations to
come. Do not offer on this altar any other incense or any
burnt offering or grain offering, and do not pour a drink
offering on it. Once a year Aaron shall make atonement
on its horns. This annual atonement must be made with
the blood of the atoning sin offering for the generations
to come. It is most holy to the LORD. (Exodus 30:7-10)

Yom Kippur literally means "day" and "atonement" and it was
the day when the high priest would sacrifice an animal on the bronze
altar to pay for his sins, the sins of all the people, and to cleanse the
tabernacle and all of its utensils and furnishings. The blood was
taken behind the veil and into the Most Holy Place by the high
priest and sprinkled on the ark of the covenant for atonement and
then brought into the Holy Place to be spread on the four horns of
the altar of incense to cleanse it. This was a day to make the entire
camp of Israel and God's dwelling place holy, clean and to restore it
to a holy and righteous state before God.

Christ and the Altar of Incense

There are many different angles from which to view the altar
of incense, and it is perhaps one of the most intriguing pieces of
furniture we have looked at so far. First, Christ is clearly seen in
both the function of this piece and in the role and function as our
High Priest as the mediator on behalf of the people at this altar.
As we saw earlier in this study, Jesus was the unblemished sacrifice
offered once and for all for our sin. Figuratively, it was His blood
that was brought from the outer courtyard into the Holy Place to
be sprinkled on this altar and then into the Most Holy Place where
it was sprinkled on the ark of the covenant.

At the same time, Jesus served as the High Priest going before the Father on our behalf with His blood. He acted as the intermediary between us and God the Father. Paul says, *"For there is one God and one mediator between God and mankind, the man Christ Jesus, who gave Himself as a ransom for all people. This has now been witnessed to at the proper time"* (1 Tim. 2:5-6). Jesus is our High Priest who mediates between God the Father and mankind so we might enter boldly into the throne room, which we will see is literally the Most Holy Place.

Second, our prayers are like the sweet smelling smoke of burning incense. Revelation 8:3-4 tells us the prayers of the saints are offered up with incense. Just as the incense on the altar was to be kept burning in the tabernacle, so our prayers are to be offered continually (1 Thess. 5:17).

Lastly, the Holy Spirit has an ongoing role in this altar as well. Jesus gave us the Holy Spirit to intercede for us before the Father. Our prayers don't end when we don't know what to say to God. Romans 8:26 says the Spirit of God intercedes for us when we don't know how to pray. We have the privilege to have the Spirit pray on our behalf when we are simply out of words. The Spirit searches out and knows our hearts and minds and can usher those requests to God on our behalf. Isn't it awesome how God has given so many different layers of symbolism in the tabernacle that we can trace forward in history to apply to our lives today?

Foundational Elements of Worship at the Altar

Prayer, Encounters with God's Spirit

The altar of incense is a place interwoven with the entire Trinity of God. It is where we experience Jesus and the Holy Spirit coming before the throne of God in heaven on our behalf. It is where we bring our lives and our hearts to offer before God. We no longer need to bring physical incense to a physical altar because a transition to the spiritual realm has already taken place.

Incense was offered daily—all day. It was to be burned unceasingly. Similarly, we are told to pray unceasingly (1 Thess. 5:17) and that our lives are the pleasing aroma of Christ before God (2 Cor. 2:15). However, we should be careful to be an offering with a fragrant scent and not a detestable one! God does not delight in the offering of incense from lives that are not living for Him (Is. 1:13). We need to test our lives with regard to the recipe of our own incense. The incense of our lives may appear to have all the right outwardly ingredients to someone else, but the quality of those ingredients must be pure, honest, righteous, and holy to be truly sweet before God. The incense of our lives matters! What does the recipe for the incense of your life and prayers include? Is it a sweet encounter with God?

Digging Deeper

The altar of incense is a very significant and special place. This is the place where we experience the Trinity of God. Picture yourself being led by the hand of Jesus on the one side and by God's Spirit on the other. Together, you approach the throne of God the Father. Jesus brings the blood He has shed on your behalf to spread on the incense altar and the Holy Spirit speaks the words of your heart which are beyond our human words. This is the altar of incense. It is the pouring out of ourselves.

There is a verse you are likely familiar with but perhaps have not had a chance to understand in the original language. *"For we are God's handiwork, created in Christ Jesus to do good works, which*

God prepared in advance for us to do" (Eph. 2:10). Look at the first phrase again: "We are God's handiwork." The original Greek word for *handiwork* is "pŏiēma" (poy-ah-mah) from which we get our word *poem*. Think about that! Your life is a poem that you and God continue to write together. As we come before the altar of incense, we need not be fancy with our words. Our lives are a poem that we can give back to God.

1. Contemplate Psalm 19:1. This is another instance of God's handiwork. What do you notice about the function of God's creation? In other words, what is creation doing? How does that compare to our function as God's people?

2. Read through 2 Corinthians 2:15-17. Do you think this was only written as an example of Paul's life and mission or can you see yourself in this passage? Should you see yourself in this passage?

3. Ponder Psalm 141:2. There is a lot of tabernacle language in this verse. What does this passage mean to you? What picture comes to mind as you picture yourself in this verse?

Our worship response: When you consider the recipe for the incense of your life, what positive and sweet smelling ingredients can you bring (e.g., honesty, trustworthiness, lovingkindness)? What negative and possibly detestable ingredients need to be washed away (e.g., selfishness, pride, arrogance)? Tap into your creativity and write a recipe card with the ingredients of the incense you bring to God. Write the directions for combining the ingredients into a prayer.

Prayer: Thank You, God for hearing my prayers! Who am I that you should give me any attention at all? And yet, You do, and You desire my attention. I fall short at times, and I know I bring detestable things along with me as I come before you. Guide me and prompt me to see those times where I need to ask for forgiveness and cleansing. Holy Spirit, thank You for bringing my prayers before the Father. I'm so grateful You know my mind and my heart when I'm at a loss before the Father. It is You who carries me along and speaks on my behalf. Thank You for such a tremendous blessing. Amen.

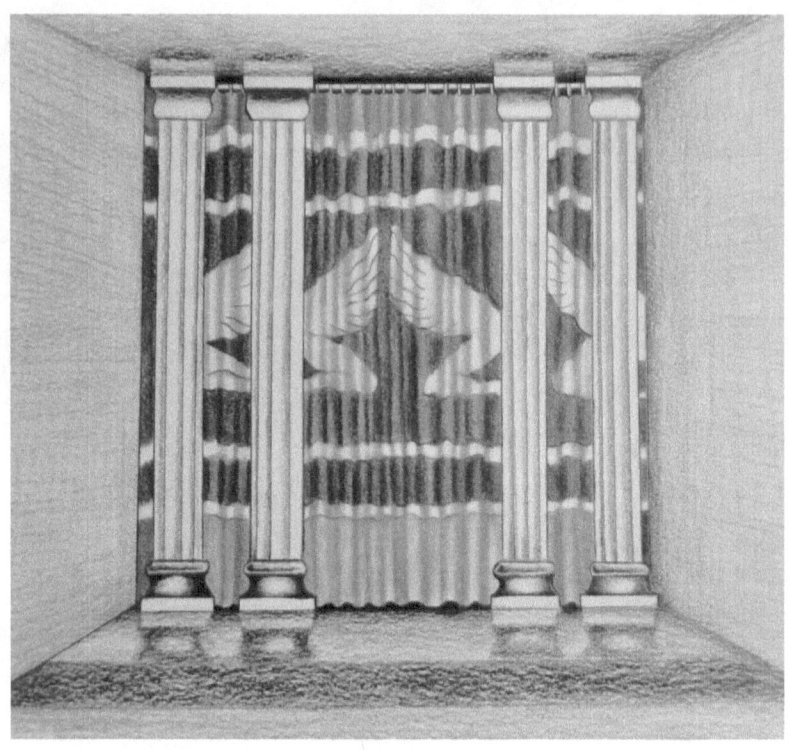

Make a curtain of blue, purple and scarlet yarn and finely twisted linen, with cherubim worked into it by a skilled craftsman. Hang it with gold hooks on four posts of acacia wood overlaid with gold and standing on four silver bases. Hang the curtain from the clasps and place the ark of the covenant law behind the curtain. The curtain will separate the Holy Place from the Most Holy Place.

(Exodus 26:31-33)

10

Most Holy Place Furnishings

---

*T*he veil was the object that provided the physical separation between sinful man and God. The Bible gives a very simple description of this curtain. It was woven from blue, purple, and scarlet yarn along with finely twisted linen. This curtain had cherubim embroidered onto it and was hung from clasps between four golden posts made of acacia wood and covered in gold. Yes, this is a theme!

The first instance we see of cherubim in the Bible is in Genesis 3:24: "After he drove the man out, he placed on the East side of the Garden of Eden cherubim and a flaming sword flashing back and forth to guard the way to the tree of life." Over and over again we see cherubim acting as guardians for God. We find cherubim on the ark of the covenant, as "decorations" in the fabric, and carved into the structure of the temple itself. In Ezekiel, cherubim play a huge role as they accompany God's glory as He departs the temple through the eastern gate.

Ezekiel had a lot to say about the entrance to the temple through the eastern gate (also called the Golden Gate, the Beautiful Gate, or Gate of Mercy). When the glory of the Lord departed the temple in Ezekiel 10 and 11, we find God's glory moving from the Most Holy Place into the Holy Place and then exiting the courtyard through the eastern gate. In chapter 11:22-23 we read that the glory of the Lord moved out of the temple complex all together and moved away and toward the East. There will be a day when we see the glory of the Lord coming from the East, reentering the eastern gate and moving back into the third temple.

Notice the pattern of worship we have been tracing thus far as it has continually moved from east to west. Although the tabernacle was a tent meant to be mobile, it is always described as having its entrance facing east with the Most Holy Place at its western most point. Perhaps when you think of these directions, the following verse comes to mind: *"as far as the east is from the west, so far has he removed our transgressions from us"* (Ps. 103:12). Take notice of the journey we have taken so far. As far as the east is (the bronze altar in the outer courtyard) from the west (Most Holy Place), that is how far it takes to remove our sins. Quite a journey and what a sweet picture!

There is an organization called the Temple Institute in Jerusalem currently preparing for the third temple. A modern day Sanhedrin is in place, many of the temple objects have been recreated, and ancient sacrificial practices are being taught to the Levites in preparation for the reinstitution of the sacrificial system. A golden menorah created in the manner of the one described previously currently stands on display in the old city of Jerusalem. We live in interesting times and I can't but wonder if perhaps the eastern gate will be visited by our Savior sooner than we may realize!

Christ and the Veil

The significance of Christ and the veil is perhaps the story we are most familiar with. It is said the veil or curtain of the temple was torn from top to bottom at the moment of Christ's death (Matt. 27:51; Mark 15:38; Luke 23:45). There are actually many different interpretations of the significance of that event.

The first interpretation says at the moment of Christ's death, the curtain was torn from top to bottom symbolizing the freedom for all mankind to enter into the Most Holy Place. With the death of Christ, the sin of man was atoned for once and for all, and there is no longer any need for separation between man and God.

Another interpretation states that the tearing was obliterating the barrier between the different status of people. There was no longer the division of the common person, the priest, or the high priest. All were made equal from God's perspective.

Still another interpretation of this event is that the tearing of the veil was symbolic of the Jewish custom of tearing one's clothes during a time of mourning. Some think this was the temple itself in mourning or God mourning the death of His Son.

All the above interpretations have some powerful symbolism. Perhaps the overall meaning is not just one interpretation but a blend. Regardless, one thing can be said most emphatically— the function of the curtain was done away with. The separation of the Holy Place from the Most Holy Place was no longer necessary.

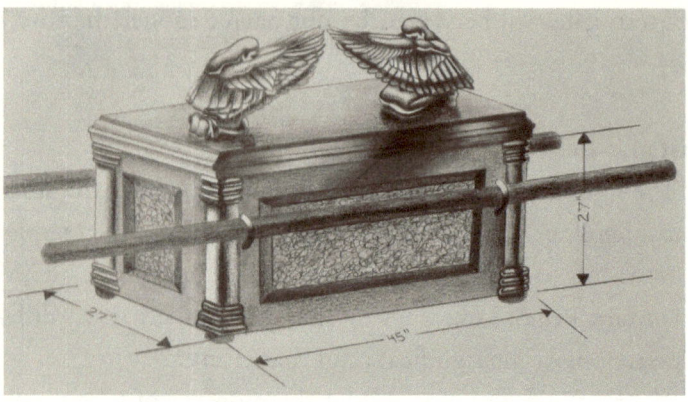

Have them make an ark of acacia wood—two and a half cubits long, a cubit and a half wide, and a cubit and a half high. Overlay it with pure gold, both inside and out, and make a gold molding around it. Cast four gold rings for it and fasten them to its four feet, with two rings on one side and two rings on the other. Then make poles of acacia wood and overlay them with gold. Insert the poles into the rings on the sides of the ark to carry it. The poles are to remain in the rings of this ark; they are not to be removed. Then put in the ark the tablets of the covenant law, which I will give you.

Make an atonement cover of pure gold—two and a half cubits long and a cubit and a half wide. And make two cherubim out of hammered gold at the ends of the cover. Make one cherub on one end and the second cherub on the other; make the cherubim of one piece with the cover, at the two ends. The cherubim are to have their wings spread upward, overshadowing the cover with them. The cherubim are to face each other, looking toward the cover. Place the cover on top of the ark and put in the ark the tablets of the covenant law that I will give you. There, above the cover between the two cherubim that are over the ark of the covenant law, I will meet with you and give you all my commands for the Israelites. (Exodus 25:10-22)

The Ark of the Covenant

The final piece in our tabernacle study is the ark of the covenant. The ark consisted of two pieces: the lid (or Mercy Seat) and the box container. This box was once again made out of acacia wood covered with gold. It was approximately forty-five inches long, twenty-seven inches wide, and twenty-seven inches deep. Pause for a moment and picture those measurements—they are about the size of a coffee table. Did you ever picture it being so small? It's such a well-known part of our Bible story and once again it's probably easier to picture it being much larger than it really was. If you look at the old 1980s movie *Raiders of the Lost Ark*, they actually seem to get these measurements pretty accurately in their depiction of the ark.

The mercy seat (or lid) rests on top of the box and is similar to the golden lampstand because it was also made of one piece of hammered gold. Two guardian cherubim were on top facing each other. They spread their wings over the center of the cover and focused their attention to this same place. In between the cherubim is where the Shekinah glory of God would be seen in two seemingly opposite traits: brilliance and smoke. The term *Shekinah* is simply a Hebrew term meaning "that which dwells" or "the one who dwells" and refers to the manifest presence of God. It was upon this Mercy Seat that the high priest would offer the atoning blood sacrifice he had brought into the Holy of Holies with him.

The ark of the covenant was far and away the most sacred place in all the tabernacle, because it was thought of as the place where heaven would literally meet earth. The ark was the footstool of God's throne in heaven. There was a unique connection between the spiritual or heavenly realm and our physical earth found in the ark of the covenant. The Holy of Holies can be described as the throne room of God. He is the King in the midst of the mighty camp of His people, and it was His throne (the footstool) in that room!

Consider this visual the next time you read or sing about being at the footstool of God's throne or bowing at His feet! Psalm 132:7-8 says: *"Let us go to his dwelling place; let us worship at his footstool— arise, LORD, and come to your resting place, you and the ark of your might."* In Psalm 99:5 we read: *"Exalt the LORD our God and worship at His footstool; he is holy."* It doesn't have to be some abstract picture; God gave us a visual description in His Scripture! Isn't it fascinating to have a visual of the link between our earthly realm and the spiritual heavenly realm of God? It is no wonder the high priest had to prepare himself for service to God. He was thought to be literally serving at God's feet!

Another profound visual is the cherubim upon the mercy seat. Remember, the cherubim are God's guardians. To be in the shelter or shadow of the Lord, or in the shelter of His wings, is to be at the mercy seat with God. What comes to mind as you read the following passages? Perhaps it will give you a new picture of being protected by the love of God:

"I long to dwell in your tent forever and take refuge in the shelter of your wings." (Psalm 61:4)

"Whoever dwells in the shelter of the Most High will rest in the shadow of the Almighty." (Psalm 91:1)

"He will cover you with his feathers, and under his wings you will find refuge." (Psalm 91:4)

Perhaps like me, you find these passages especially comforting as you picture yourself in that special place on the mercy seat being taken care of by God Himself along with His royal guardian cherubim. Oh, I long to be under the shadow of the wings—a place of deep intimacy with our Father in heaven!

Christ and the Ark

As fascinating as it is to think of God's throne literally stretching from heaven to earth, we must remember we also see the life of Jesus as the Person where heaven and earth meet. God's manifest presence was not in the Holy of Holies in the temple of Jerusalem two thousand years ago because He was outside the temple walking, talking, teaching, and healing His people!

There were three items originally placed in the ark that have significance as well: a jar of manna, Aaron's budded staff, and the tables of the law or ten commandments. Each of them demonstrate some aspect of Jesus' relationship to us.

Manna was God's provision for the Israelites in the wilderness. It was literally bread from heaven to sustain them in the desert (John 6:31, Ex. 16:32-36). Manna was provided by God every day for forty years while they traveled to the promised land. So how does Jesus represent this? Jesus said He is the bread of life (John 6:25-59). He is our manna from heaven. He is God's provision to us as we journey through life to our promised land in heaven!

Aaron's budded staff represents God's chosen priestly line. Numbers 17 tells the story of Aaron's staff budding through supernatural circumstances as a testimony to God's choice for Him as the high priest of Israel. God made it clear that He is the only one who chooses who will lead His people. And Jesus? Isaiah spoke of the Chosen One who was to come (Is. 53). The Gospels also record the testimony of God making it clear that Jesus is the Chosen One, the Savior, Messiah, and Son of God.

The tables of the law or the ten commandments represent God's instruction—His word to us. These were tablets of stone inscribed by the divine hand of God. John 1 tells us Jesus is the Word. "For the law was given through Moses; grace and truth came through Jesus Christ" (John 1:17). The law is fulfilled in the person of Jesus Christ!

These three things together were the evidence and legal testimony to God's saving and preserving His people. Jesus embodies all of these things. Isn't this God whom we worship truly amazing?!

Foundational Elements of Worship in the Most Holy Place

Freedom, Intimacy

We've spent a great deal of time looking at the necessity of being cleansed and holy before God. We've spent time looking at how we are to relate to one another in fellowship, and on mission. Now we have the opportunity to revel in the relationship we have with God. We can go to that place where few had the opportunity to go in ancient Israel: the Most Holy Place. We can boldly go up to the throne of God because of Jesus Christ. Each and every one of us!

> Therefore, brothers (sisters), since we have confidence to enter the Most Holy Place by the blood of Jesus, by a new and living way opened for us through the curtain, that is, his body, and since we have a great priest over the house of God, let us draw near to God with a sincere heart and with the full assurance that faith brings, having our

hearts sprinkled to cleanse us from a guilty conscience
and having our bodies washed with pure water.
(Hebrews 10:19-22)

Think about this for a moment. During the days of the
tabernacle, Aaron was the high priest over all of God's people. He
was allowed to enter into the presence of God only once a year.
Through Jesus our High Priest, however, we have the opportunity
to be in God's presence whenever we want. Talk about freedom and
privilege. We don't have to wait for one special day each year! In
fact, God desires our attention each and every day. He loves us and
wants us to spend time reading His Word, sharing our hearts with
Him and being open to learning from Him.

Consider the relationship you have with a loved one, a spouse
or close friend. Do you waltz into their presence once a week, declare
what a great person they are, maybe tell them your misgivings from
the week and then say, "see ya next week!"? Most likely not! We
spend time sitting down and hearing from them, sharing our own
thoughts and feelings with them, laughing or crying together, or
enjoying a meal with them. We may often link the term *intimacy*
with marriage or with a sexual connotation. The dictionary
simply describes *intimacy* as a close familiarity with another or a
comfortable friendship. When we share an intimate relationship
with someone, there is closeness and comfort with that person you
probably don't have with just anyone. This is the kind of intimacy
God wants with us. He wants us to feel comfortable with Him and
close enough to Him that we will follow wherever He wants us to
go. Although the journey may not always be comfortable, we can
worship Him with freedom from fear and have peace in our hearts
that He is for us no matter who may stand against us.

Digging Deeper

Have you ever stopped to picture what the temple may have looked like inside on the day of the crucifixion when the veil was torn? The ark of the covenant and God's manifest presence was no longer present in the Holy of Holies at the time of Christ. For many years during the time of Christ, the high priest would have been going behind the veil to an empty Holy of Holies on the Day of Atonement. God was not there. He was walking around in the streets as the person of Jesus Christ!

When Jesus died on the cross the priests were probably tending to their daily duties in the temple as usual when suddenly the massive curtain split from the top down. The curtain in the temple was as tall as a three story building and torn, not from the bottom up by man but from the top down by God. Picture the horror of those Jewish priests who saw this happen. The Most Holy Place was laid open to all priests at that point, and God was not there! Remember, only the high priest had the privilege to see inside this sacred space and only once each year, and yet there it was for all the priests to see! They must have been terrified and perhaps went running for their lives since the punishment would normally be death for intruding on this space.

The Bible does not record what happened after this, but the temple remained standing and functioning from Christ's death between the early AD 30s until AD 70 when it was destroyed by the Romans. It's not hard to imagine the curtain was either stitched back together or more likely a new curtain was made and hung in its place. Think of the symbolic significance, and yet are we any different?

There are times in my life where I have tried to put separation back between me and God. My husband and I suffered greatly from infertility and miscarriages, and I was downright angry with God. That was definitely a very dark season of my life where I kept God at arm's length. I did not completely walk away from my faith, but I was quite content to have a veil or curtain in place. It felt comfortable to keep the veil of my heart stitched closed against God.

When we turn away from God and try to "do" life on our own, it's as if we stitch the veil back together and hang it right back up. What areas of your life are you trying to handle on your own? What areas of your life are you trying to fix on your own? In what areas of life have you tried to stitch the veil? Remember, beloved, your God tore the veil down! You can live in freedom and not in confinement. We have the amazing privilege to live as part of God's royal priesthood and can be bold before the throne of God no matter our circumstances (Heb. 10:19)! He wants us to worship Him with all of who we are: body, soul, mind and spirit (Luke 10:27; Mark 12:30). He wants a close, intimate, personal friendship with you. He has made the way available by the tearing of the veil through the sacrifice of His Son. He is big enough to handle your anger, your frustrations, your hurts, and your sorrows. Have you responded to His intimate gesture of care and love?

1. Read through 1 Kings 6:23-37 and Ezekiel 10-11. What more can you learn about the cherubim, the guardian creatures of God we see all over the tabernacle and temple?

2.   Read through Leviticus 16:1-34 to see the process the high
       priest had to go through before entering the Holy of Holies.
       Summarize the ritual in your own words. Is there anything
       intentional you do when coming before our Holy God?

3.   Read Numbers 16-17. Some of the Israelites began to grumble
       about the position Moses and Aaron had in relation to the
       people and with God. The leaders felt all people were holy
       and challenged the authority of Moses and Aaron. How did
       their jealousy get the better of them? Why do you think God
       didn't just allow everyone to go through the ritual cleaning and
       enter into the Holy of Holies in the tabernacle whenever they
       wanted to?

Our worship response: Consider this amazing gift of eternal life
and the intimate relationship with the God of the universe you've
been given. Do something life-giving as an offering of thanksgiving
to God for this gift. You might bring fresh life to your soul as you
spend time in song on a walk in God's creation. You can plant some
seeds or offer life-giving words of encouragement to someone who
needs them today. Be creative!

Prayer: Thank you, Father, for the privilege I have to have an
intimate relationship with You. I don't have to go to a particular
place to worship you; I have you in my heart! You have told me
in Scripture I am a living temple. You no longer live in a physical

temple. You live in me. Understanding that fact is both humbling and overwhelming. Those high priests had so many instructions to make themselves acceptable and clean so they might be near Your presence and here I am. I have Your divine presence within me as Your living temple! I'm not worthy and yet You love me enough to live within my heart. Thank you for such a tremendous blessing and helping me live in a manner worthy of Your presence in my life. Amen.

11

Worshiping Through God's Blueprint

---

*U*p to this point, we've been focused on each aspect of the tabernacle complex. We have looked intently at the blueprint God gave us for heavenly worship and carefully studied the holy objects and the symbolism found in each. It's now time to fly up to thirty thousand feet and see how this blueprint flows together in our own spiritual lives. From here we can see the overall *spiritual* blueprint God laid out in the physical tabernacle.

I began this book by saying there are some foundational elements or truths God laid out in the directions given for creating the tabernacle. As we encounter each of these things with God, we can worship Him with the worship language we already have. In other words, do you sing? Sing about God's holiness. Do you paint? Paint about being washed clean. Do you minister to others in need? Share your testimony of being in right standing with God. Do you write poetry? Write about being at the footstool of God's

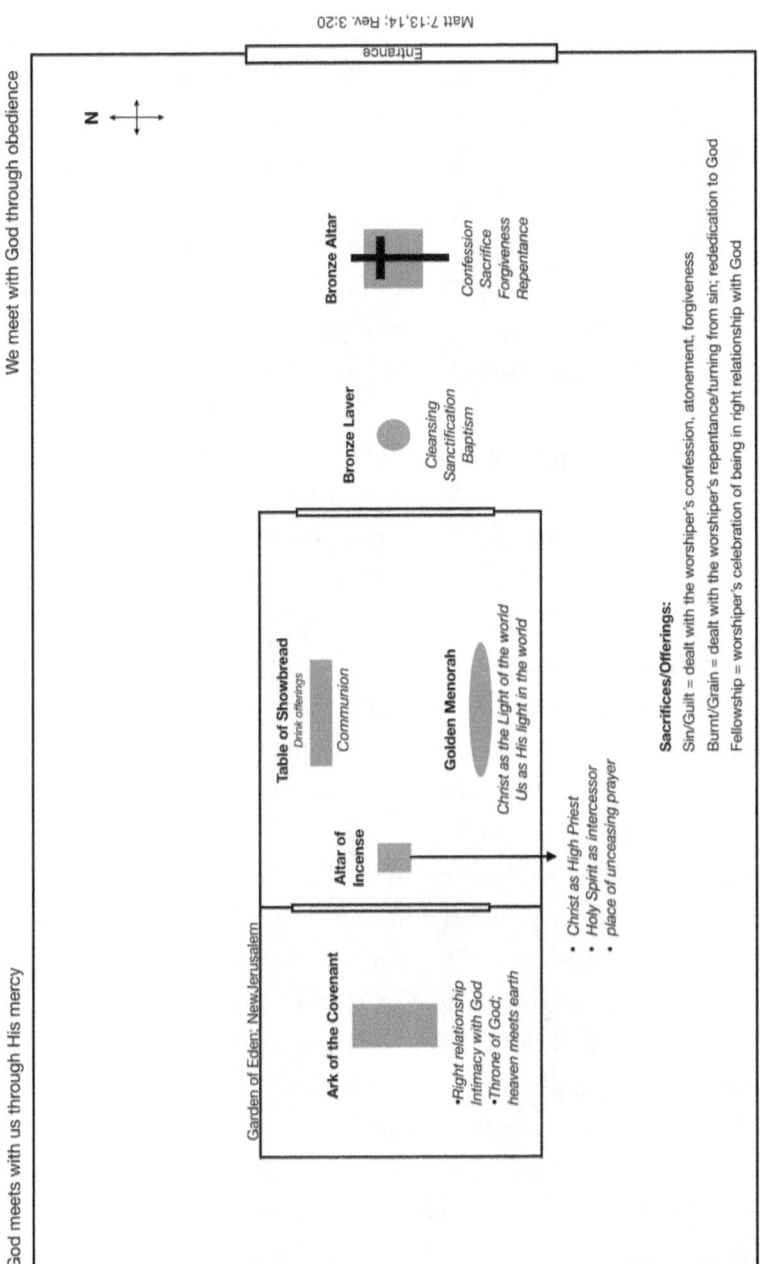

Matt 7:13,14; Rev. 3:20

Entrance

N

We meet with God through obedience

God meets with us through His mercy

Bronze Altar

Confession
Sacrifice
Forgiveness
Repentance

Bronze Laver

Cleansing
Sanctification
Baptism

Garden of Eden; New Jerusalem

Table of Showbread
Drink offerings

Communion

Golden Menorah

Christ as the Light of the world
Us as His light in the world

Altar of Incense

- *Christ as High Priest*
- *Holy Spirit as intercessor*
- *place of unceasing prayer*

Ark of the Covenant

•*Right relationship*
Intimacy with God
•*Throne of God;*
heaven meets earth

Sacrifices/Offerings:

Sin/Guilt = dealt with the worshiper's confession, atonement, forgiveness

Burnt/Grain = dealt with the worshiper's repentance/turning from sin; rededication to God

Fellowship = worshiper's celebration of being in right relationship with God heavenly throne or what it means to be a light in our dark world. Do you enjoy studying? Go deeper into Scripture about sanctification or understanding God's beauty. The possibilities are endless! Part of worship is also to simply acknowledge, accept, and agree with what God has already offered to us and then respond with some expression of worship. No need to be fancy. Simply respond back to God when you encounter Him and His truth.

In previous chapters, I gave you many prompts for further study and worship. Now that we have come to the end of our study, feel free to go back and revisit those things allowing the Holy Spirit to lead you deeper into Scripture. You may find you only want to ponder one aspect a day or even focus your attention on one aspect over several days. That's up to you. Be as creative as you want to be!

Sharing the Tabernacle

So where else can we go from here? Don't just internalize what you've read, I would encourage you to teach others. Being a teacher was never on my radar, but when I went to Israel for the first time, God gave me a passion for the tabernacle and now I just can't be quiet about it. I want others to see Christ in the *whole* Bible! The Old Testament is connected intimately with the New Testament, but often we simply need to do a little work to see it.

I had the opportunity to go to a national park in Israel called Timnah Park and this is where the seeds of passion were sown into my heart. It was a very simple park in the middle of the desert of Israel where a tabernacle had been constructed to the correct dimensions given in the Bible. I was fascinated to see how small it really was and to see the type of landscape where it would have been pitched.

When I came home from Israel, I wanted to share that eye-opening experience with others. A small group at the church where I had been working decided to create its own tabernacle to share with the people of the church as an interactive and introspective Good Friday open house experience. We didn't have enough space to lay it out as it would have been originally, but we created stations anyway for people to walk through and a booklet to take along the way to instruct them as to the use of each object.

During that Good Friday event, we had an experience together as a church that can only be described as holy. Everyone was asked to remain quiet and walk through the various stations and fellowship with God alone. We had a bronze altar station with votive candles for people to light and lay their confessions on the altar. We had a wash basin where they could pour water over their hands as a symbolic gesture of cleansing. At the table of showbread, we set out bread and juice so the worshipers could receive communion. We asked people to write out their prayers at the altar of incense, which they could then pin to the curtain inside the holy of holies.

People felt they had come to a holy place and even came to the point of removing their shoes before entering the holy of holies that we had set up. There were others who sat in various places in our tabernacle for a long time to simply spend some intimate time of worship with God. It was reflective, highly personal, and simply a wonderful experience—in spite of the accidental fireball we had fly out of our bronze altar! At first I think some wondered if God had met us quite personally in that fireball, but a little search on the Internet about putting out a candle wax fire with water should shed some light on our little dilemma.

God's blueprint for worship is meant to be experienced. It's not something just to read about. I hope that you will take your church through a tabernacle experience too. No matter what your role in the church is or the resources you have available, I believe God will meet you and your church very personally as you attempt to reconstruct His home—one He designed for you to experience. Here are a few prompts to contemplate that might help you come up with ideas that will work for your church:

- First and foremost, use this material as a worship team study or devotional. I can't stress this enough. There are too many churches out there that have great musicians and wonderful worship leaders who have no formal biblical or theological training in the area of worship. I've learned firsthand that many seminaries also fail to educate pastors on worship theology as well. This makes for a *wonderful* survey for your worship team (as well as your pastoral team), and it will give them the biblical and theological background they should know for what they do each week while they lead your congregation. This will help them understand heaven's blueprint for worship—that we should all be connected to.

- Create a space for your congregation to walk through. Engaging the senses helps us connect with and retain information better. Set up stations (e.g., a bronze altar station, bronze laver, table of showbread, golden menorah, altar of incense, ark of the covenant) and give instruction to the people who walk through your tabernacle. That may come in the form of a teacher at each station to explain what that object is for and to be available to answer questions or perhaps an instruction booklet using the sample service in the next chapter as a guide to hand out so they can walk through your tabernacle silently.

- Consider having your creative team build a replica of each of the objects to go along with your sermons. At the end of your series, bring all of those pieces of furniture together and set them up somewhere in your church for people to walk through and experience— maybe even on your stage area if it's large enough. The possibilities are endless, and a creative team will enjoy recreating this heavenly worship pattern. Pull them together, turn them loose, and see what they come up with.

- Take some of the ideas above and create one single special service with a physical walk-through afterward. There are so many creative ways to use this material with your church. Bring the artists, the musicians, those with a passion for worship, the creative thinkers, and the pastors together and do a little brainstorming. The result might blow your socks off!

- Use this material as a multi-week small group series with your women's or men's groups, or even as a group of church staff and pastors. You can meet and study each object individually over the course of many weeks or you can group them into two meetings: one on the context of the tabernacle, the outer courtyard and the objects there and the other on the tabernacle tent and the objects in it.

- Pull some other churches in your neighborhood together to do one of the above ideas. It's a great way

to fellowship with other believers and get to know the
other churches in your area.

Be creative. Have fun and engage your people! You will be
amazed at the result.

Your turn!

Now that you've had a chance to walk through the tabernacle
personally, I challenge you to do it again . . . and again and again!
Find your own creative ways to respond in worship. Remember, this
is *God's* heavenly blueprint for worship. This process of becoming
more holy and Christlike is by His design. This is not something
you walk through once and call it good. In order to continue the
sanctification process, it must be walked again and again; each
time with more experience and more Christlike attitudes. It is
kind of like the "two steps forward, one step back" principle. The
idea is that we continue to grow more Christlike while knowing
at times we screw up and need to start again. Hopefully we don't
fall back as far as we once did, and the lessons we learn from our
sin continue to propel us into being a more holy and Christlike
priesthood.

I think the most amazing thing about this entire study is to
realize the access we have as believers to the God of the universe.
It's incredibly humbling. We know the tabernacle had a myriad of
priests who tended to the things of God, and yet only one of those
many priests had the privilege to go into the Holy of Holies and
actually encounter God in a way no other person could. Only one
priest in the thousands of Israelites in the desert had the privilege to
experience the tabernacle to its fullest: to sacrifice and confess, to be

cleansed and forgiven, to enter into worship and encounter the true and living God. Only one person had the privilege to experience the tabernacle in all it was designed for.

Now we live under a new covenant in New Testament times and guess what? If you have accepted Christ into your life, you are that one person! Do you feel as blessed as you really are? As a Christ follower, we have the opportunity to be in God's presence twenty-four seven to sacrifice and confess, to be cleansed and forgiven, to worship and encounter the true and living God! In fact, we *are* the dwelling place of God! He is already dwelling within us. The apostle Paul wrote: "Don't you know that you yourselves are God's temple and that God's Spirit lives in you?" (1 Cor 3:16). We don't need to *go* anywhere, because we *are* the living temple of our Holy God.

If you ever doubt God loves you, look at all He has done for you. From the garden of Eden, He created a way to live with man. Man messed up and He again created a way through the tabernacle and then the temple. And then God sent His Son, Jesus Christ to make a way once again. This time, Christ's sacrifice became the permanent solution for God to dwell with man and vice versa. Over and over again, God continued to work with our screwups in order that we might still live in community with Him. We did none of the above. It was all God's doing. He loved us enough to go to great lengths throughout history to be with us. We simply need to accept this gift He has given us. It is our job to remember and respond to God's grand gesture of love for us.

*If I had understood then, as I do now, how this great King
really dwells within this little palace of my soul, I should not*

have left Him alone so often, but should have stayed with Him and never have allowed His dwelling-place to get so dirty. How wonderful it is that He Whose greatness could fill a thousand worlds should confine Himself within so small a space. . . . Being the Lord, He has, of course, perfect freedom, and, as He loves us, He fashions Himself to our measure.

— Teresa of Avila
Way of Perfection

12

A Sample Tabernacle Service

This chapter is intended to give you some specifics that you can use for a service, a sermon, or special group study. You can move through the entire thing in one session or take your time and move through one section at a time and take more time to dive deeper. Each section contains the following prompts to start you out. Don't feel you need to follow these sections exactly. They are simply meant to spur you on to being creative for the body of believers God has given to you to shepherd:

1. Instruction: This section gives a brief overview about each section of the tabernacle. It can be read as is or used to prompt you in your own instruction.

2. Sharing Scripture: The reading of Scripture is a great way to involve other people in your group. You can either have these pre-printed and handed out to various people in your group to read, have them projected in a PowerPoint or Keynote presentation for the congregation to read together, or enlist your leaders to take turns reading these passages.

3. Prayer Prompts: Feel free to use the prayer prompts for free-flowing, spoken congregational prayer or introspective personal prayer. You can have people come together in smaller groups for free-flowing prayer if the congregation is too large.

4. Song Themes: I provide some suggested themes that will work well for each section. Check out Christian Copyright Licensing International's website songselect.ccli.com for a huge list of songs separated by theme and topic. Use my list simply as a prompt to do some digging through your church music and pull up the songs that would resonate with your congregation.

Section 1:

INTRODUCTION

1. Instruction: The tabernacle was the dwelling place of God as He led His people through the wilderness to the promised land. The writer of Hebrews tells us that it was a copy and shadow of what is already in heaven (Heb. 8:5). That is why God instructed Moses saying: "See to it that you make everything according to the pattern shown you on the mountain" (Ex. 25:40). As we understand the tabernacle, we come to see Jesus in all aspects of it and the pattern of worship that God intended for us.

The tabernacle, and the temple by extension, was the central place of worship for God's people. In it, we learn about invitation, sacrifice, repentance, atonement, holiness, baptism, communion, and so on. These are the foundational elements of worship. When we have an experience or an encounter with God we come to understand these things in fresh ways. We then express our worship through things like prayer, meditation, acts of service, song, and dance as a result. Together, we will walk through the pattern of worship that God established through the tabernacle and see how the life and ministry of Christ fulfilled many of the aspects of the tabernacle. Peter says, "you are a chosen people, a royal priesthood, a holy nation, God's special possession, that you may declare the praises of him who called you out of darkness into his wonderful light" (1 Pet 2:9). So fellow priests, let's enter in and begin!

2. Sharing Scripture: John 1:1, 14

3. Prayer Prompts: Take a moment to greet the Holy Spirit in your life. Welcome Him to guide your day and minister to you in the areas that need His touch.

4. Song Themes: Invitation, Dwelling, Presence, Journey

Section 2:

OUTER COURTYARD — INVITATION

1. Instruction: The outer courtyard is a place of invitation. It was a very simple fence of white linen in a rectangle with an opening on the eastern side of the structure to enter through. Bronze and silver posts and bases were made to hold the white linen fence upright. For some perspective, the outer fence was approximately one-quarter the size of an NFL football field. It would extend from the goal line to the twenty-five yard line at its width and from sideline to sideline for its length. There is one entrance, a small "gate" of linen on the eastern side. In this entrance we see Christ calling us to come and begin the journey to the Most Holy Place with Him. *"Ask and it will be given to you; seek and you will find; knock and the door will be opened to you"* (Matt. 7:7).

2. Sharing Scripture: Matthew 7:13-14; Revelation 3:20

3. Prayer Prompts: Acknowledge that Jesus is the only way to the Father. Thank Him for the privilege you have to enter into His presence.

4. Song Themes: Invitation, Processional, Courtyard, Expectation

Section 3:

BRONZE ALTAR – REPENTANCE, FORGIVENESS

1. Instruction: In Old Testament times, we would have entered into the courtyard and quickly been made aware of our sinful nature at the bronze altar. It is at this altar that the priests would offer daily sacrifices, including those for the atonement of sin. It's important to realize that the life of the sacrificial animal was taken by the worshipper and not the priests. It was their responsibility because it was their sin that had to be dealt with. They were to lay their hand on the head of the animal to symbolically transfer their sins to the atoning animal and then take the life of the animal with the other. It was a gruesome and bloody process, and the people were well aware of the cost of their sin.

It is at this altar we also see the cross of Jesus Christ. Just like the goat or the sheep, Jesus was symbolically sacrificed at this altar, giving His life as our atoning sacrifice. Unlike the goat or the sheep, He went willingly and without prompting from us. He laid his life down on this altar so that we might have our sins washed away. It is here we experience sacrifice, repentance, and forgiveness.

2. Sharing Scripture: Psalm 51:16-17; Hebrews 9:12-14; 10:11-13

3. Prayer Prompts: Pause and take a moment to confess any sin and thank God for His gift of forgiveness.

4. Song Themes: Confession, Repentance, Forgiveness, Acceptance, Obedience, Altar, Cross, Salvation

Section 4:

BRONZE LAVER – BAPTISM, SANCTIFICATION

1. Instruction: When we experience the bronze laver to the fullest, we also experience cleansing, baptism, and an understanding of our sanctification process. The priests washed their hands and feet with water in a laver described as being made of mirrors (or highly polished bronze) before entering into the tabernacle. It was an important step in their sanctification process before they would dare to move closer to God. This was a place of cleansing—where the blood of the sacrifice was washed away. As a result, the priest was considered cleansed, pure, and holy to do his ministry further in the tabernacle. When we consider what happened at the bronze laver, it's easy to see the parallel to our own baptism in Christ. As we are baptized, our old life is washed away, and we are born into a new life in Christ. (*This is a great opportunity to baptize those wishing to be baptized.*)

2. Sharing Scripture: Psalm 51:1-2; Acts 2:38

3. Prayer Prompts: Take a moment and ask God to cleanse you and make you holy. Thank Him for that cleansing and for your baptism into His family. Ask for direction and guidance as you seek to be holy and set apart for Him.

4. Song Themes: Holiness, Sanctification, Baptism, Cleansing, Restoration, Water, River, Refreshing, Purity

Section 5:

HOLY PLACE: TABLE OF SHOWBREAD COMMUNION, FELLOWSHIP

1. Instruction: As we enter the tabernacle tent, we encounter the golden table of showbread on our right. Here we experience communion and fellowship. On this table we would see plates, dishes, bowls, and jars for the drink offerings (Num. 4:7). Twelve loaves of bread, representing the twelve tribes of Israel, were placed here each Sabbath. They were consumed by the priests the following Sabbath. It was here that drink offerings of wine were also poured out. With the symbolism of both the bread and the wine, we realize that we experience communion at this table with God and with each other. Just as the bread was pierced and striped in its baking process and the grapes were crushed for their juice, our Lord, the Bread of Life, also was pierced, striped, and crushed for us. *(This is a great opportunity to have a communion service or even a brief communion service followed by a potluck meal.)*

2. Sharing Scripture: Isaiah 53:5; John 6:33, 51

3. Prayer Prompts: Express your gratitude to God for the fellowship and communion you have with other saints. Praise God for the beautiful visuals He gave us in the bread and the wine to remember what Jesus did for us. Share with Jesus what those visuals mean to you.

4. Song Themes: Communion, Bread of Life, Remembrance, Provision, Fellowship, Community

Section 6:

HOLY PLACE:
MENORAH – LIGHT, MISSION

1. Instruction: Directly across from the table was the golden menorah, the only light in the tabernacle tent. It is described as a tree (with buds and branches) and is meant to remind us of the trees in both the garden of Eden and the New Jerusalem—God's garden temples. The lamps were lit from sundown to sunup every day and burned a pure oil that caused no smoke. That light represents both Christ and us! Christ is the pure light of the world and does not cause the smoke of confusion or create a light that is dim. Just as that pure light of Christ shines for us, it shines in us too as He calls us to be light to the world around us. We are to be a light to the nations and extend God's kingdom to the ends of the earth. (*This is a great time to honor the stories and testimonies of your congregation as they engage their community. It is also an opportunity to honor and share the stories of missionaries your church supports.*)

2. Sharing Scripture: John 8:12; Matthew 5:14-16; Matthew 28:18-20; Ephesians 5:8-10

3. Prayer Prompts: Offer thanksgiving that you have become a part of God's family and ask the Holy Spirit to guide you as you seek to share Christ in the world around you.

4. Song Themes: Light of the world, Great Commission, Calling, Witness

Section 7:

HOLY PLACE: GOLDEN ALTAR OF INCENSE – PRAYERS, HOLY SPIRIT

1. Instruction: The last object in the Holy Place is the golden altar of incense. When we understand this altar, we understand our prayer life. This altar was the last place the high priest would attend before entering into the Holy of Holies. A special blend of incense was burned on this altar continuously. It was a unique and sacred blend that was pleasing to the Lord and not to be used for selfish reasons. Just like the incense that was burned without fail day and night, we are encouraged to pray continually or without ceasing. God desires our fellowship and the incense of our prayers. He desires to hear from us continually as we look to trust Him.

2. Sharing Scripture: 1 Thessalonians 5:16-18; Revelation 8:3-4

3. Prayer Prompts: Acknowledge the work the Holy Spirit does on your behalf. Ask God to show you the incense of your life that is pleasing and to convict you of the things that need to be changed. Ask for prompts from the Holy Spirit to rejoice always and pray continually, even when life gets busy.

4. Song Themes: Holy Spirit, Prayer, Gratitude, Thanksgiving, God's voice, Presence

Section 8:

MOST HOLY PLACE/HOLY OF HOLIES – THRONE ROOM OF GOD

1. Instruction: The Most Holy Place is the innermost room of the tabernacle. In ancient Israel, the camp of Israel would have been seen in a similar manner as other pagan military camps. The difference was that the God of Israel was the commander of the Hebrew camp. His royal room, and the place of His throne, was found in the Most Holy Place. No one was allowed to enter this room, except the designated high priest—and even then he was allowed to be in the presence of God only once per year. When the time for the new covenant came, God did away with the separation and made a way for all people to be in His presence.

Imagine the experience of the priests serving in the temple on the day that Jesus was crucified. Up to that point in time, the veil had been the division between a holy God and unholy man. On that particular day, however, the priests were undoubtedly carrying on with their daily duties in the Holy Place when the veil that separated them from the Holy of Holies was suddenly destroyed before their eyes. They were mostly likely terrified since anyone who was unqualified to enter the Holy of Holies would be struck dead. At the same time, how sad it is to stop and realize that this barrier that God removed was most likely put right back into place since the ministry of the temple continued for another almost forty years after the death of Christ.

2. Sharing Scripture: 2 Chronicles 5:7-14; Hebrews 10:19-22; Revelation 21

3. Prayer Prompts: We have been given a tremendous blessing to be in the presence of God all the time. We don't need to *go* someplace special to be with God. He is present within us and desires an intimate relationship with us. Offer words of reverence to God for this incredible blessing—that He lives inside of us.

4. Song Themes: Presence, Dwelling, King, Holiness, Worship at the throne of God, Blessings, Reverence

Section 9:

HOLY OF HOLIES: ARK OF THE COVENANT—GOD'S PRESENCE, INTIMACY

1. Instruction: The Most Holy Place contained the ark of the covenant, which is by far the most fascinating piece of furniture. There is certainly great mystery as to what happened to the ark, but there is also mystery in what it was. It was the place where God's Shekinah glory (manifest presence) rested between the cherubim on the mercy seat (or cover of the ark). It was also thought to be the very literal footstool of the throne of heaven! When we read of worshiping at or bowing down before the throne of God, this is the place they were talking about. This was the place where heaven and earth met in a mysterious way. God desires to dwell with His people. That fact has remained from the book of Genesis and will last through the fulfillment of the book of Revelation.

Inside the ark, we find many parallels between the objects there and Christ. We are told Jesus is the Word who was in the beginning, and the ark held God's written word in the form of the tablets of the commandments. Likewise, Jesus is the Bread of Life and the ark held some of the manna from the wilderness as a reminder that our life and provision comes from God. Jesus is also God's chosen High Priest who ministers for us just as the ark held Aaron's budded rod—a symbol of God's choosing who will serve as High Priest among his people. All three of these items in the ark served as a testimony to God's involvement in and provision for His people.

2. Sharing Scripture: Psalm 132:7-9; Hebrews 9:6-12; Hebrews 10:19-22

3. Prayer Prompts: Picture worshiping at the footstool of God's throne. The ark of the covenant is the footstool in the royal throne room of the tabernacle—the Holy of Holies. Offer words of worship and praise to your heavenly King at the footstool of His throne.

4. Song Themes: Reverence, Submission, Presence, Holy of Holies, Grace, God Incarnate, Footstool, Intimacy

BIBLIOGRAPHY

Alexander, T. Desmond. *From Eden to the New Jerusalem: An Introduction to Biblical Theology*. Grand Rapids, MI: Kregel Academic & Professional, 2009.

Alexander, T. Desmond. *Heaven on Earth:* Carlisle: Paternoster, 2004.

Beale, G. K., and Mitchell Kim. *God Dwells Among Us: Expanding Eden to the Ends of the Earth*. Nottingham: IVP, 2015.

Beale, Gregory K. *The Temple and the Church's Mission: a Biblical Theology of the Dwelling Place of God*. Leicester: Apollow, 2005.

Best, Harold M. *Unceasing Worship: Biblical Perspectives on Worship and the Arts*. Downers Grove, IL: InterVarsity Press, 2003.

Hegg, Tim. *The Letter Writer: Paul's Background and Torah Perspective*. Israel: First Fruits of Zion, 2002.

Lancaster, D. Thomas. *Grafted In: Israel, Gentiles, and the Mystery of the Gospel*. Marshfield, MO: First Fruits of Zion, 2009.

Peterson, David. *Engaging with God a Biblical Theology of Worship*. Downers Grove, Ill: InterVarsity Press, 2004.

Pierce, Timothy M., and E. Ray. Clendenen. *Enthroned on Our Praise: an Old Testament Theology of Worship*. Nashville, TN: B & H Academic, 2008.

Price, Randall. *Rose Guide to the Temple*. Torrance, CA: Rose Publishing, 2012.

Rose Guide to the Tabernacle. Torrance, CA: Rose Publishing , 2008.

Sabo, Michael Frank. *The Life I Want in Christ*. Micahel Frank Sabo, 1996.